Divine
INTERVENTION
CONFESSIONS OF A PASTOR

JERRY MOSES

DIVINE INTERVENTION
Copyright © 2025 by Jerry Moses

Paperback: 979-8-9935995-0-2

CONTENTS

ACKNOWLEDGEMENTS

I am very happy to endorse the life of Rev Jerry Moses. Jerry is a man who is totally sold out to Jesus. I have know him for over 13 years and have never once questioned his honesty or dedication. He had endured many hardships, but has always come out a winner. If there were more dedicated Christians like Jerry the world would be a better place. His key phrase is always, "it's all about Jesus, He is my life and my hope."

Dr R Bruce Strom, D.D.and Ph.D

Jerry Moses is a rare individual. He is a graduate of a major University and a long time employee of the Christian Broadcasting Network. I only know of one other person who has that combination of experience besides me and that is Dr. John Gilman of Dayspring Intl. Jerry is maybe the funniest (if that is a word) person I've ever been around. He has a contagious love for the Lord and for others that draws people to him. What a weapon of righteousness for Jesus! Someone who is the life of the party but wants the party to glorify Jesus!

Sincerly,

Dr. Bob Statler

I recall the time, place, and atmosphere when I first met this mighty man of God, Jerry Moses. He was teaching a group of people about the mighty "power of God." And, for those of us who know Jerry, he can be very dramatic, funny and encouraging...all at the same time, but this conversation ushered in a different atmosphere. It surely held my attention along with many others. Since that day, many years ago, I knew The Spirit of the Lord resided in this man, and he had much more to do for THE KINGDOM, before going Home. I am honored to be a part of his life and book. He has pushed through many trials and never lost his sight of WHO he belongs to. Though his armor is bent and stained, his feet still stand on solid ground. "Our anchor holds, and grips the solid Rock...this Rock is Jesus, Yes, He's the One!"

Dr. Gabriel Hope

DEDICATION

First, I want to thank The Lord Jesus Christ for His grace and mercy extended to me in numerous occasions in my life. If it were not for the guidance and comfort of the Holy Spirit, where would I be? The LOVE of my Heavenly Father has carried me when I was unlovable, and felt hopeless. He sent me my precious beautiful gorgeous wife Carol in whom I want to dedicate this book to. Then to my precious mother who loved me unconditionally, and always encouraged me. And to my loving sister and her family. And to my amazing four children and spouses. They have given us grandchildren to be proud of, and they ALL love and serve the Lord! I am very pleased with the beautiful family God has blessed me with, and I dedicate this book to all of them.

FOREWORD

The Bridge Builder

By Will Allen Dromgoole

An old man going a lone highway,

Came, at the evening cold and gray,

To a chasm vast and deep and wide.

Through which was flowing a sullen tide

The old man crossed in the twilight dim,

The sullen stream had no fear for him;

But he turned when safe on the other side

And built a bridge to span the tide.

"Old man," said a fellow pilgrim near,

"You are wasting your strength with building here:

Your journey will end with the ending day,

You never again will pass this way;

You've crossed the chasm, deep and wide,

Why build this bridge at evening tide?"

The builder lifted his old gray head;
"Good friend, in the path I have come," he said,
"There followed after me today
A youth whose feet must pass this way.
This chasm that has been as naught to me
To that fairhaired youth may a pitfall be;
He, too, must cross in the twilight dim;
Good friend, I am building this bridge for him!"

A This poem was given to me by a pastor mentor. He is now in glory and I still recall all of the amazing teachings he so graciously walked me through in the first stages of my ministry. I pray this book, much like this poem will be a bridge for many.

Chapter 1

THE FIGHT OF THE INNOCENT

12 noon

Band Room

God has not given us a spirit of fear but of power of Love and of a sound mind 2 Tim 1:7

Life is a continual transition. I think all of us have had times in our lives when we wanted time to stay in that continuum, because it seemed that everything was right. But there comes a transitional period for most of us, and they come in endless packages. Some transitions, stink like a cow barn, others smell like a rose garden. Some come in sorrow and pain, others come as joy unspeakable. When anyone looks back on their life no matter what age they are, they will see numerous changes, from beginning to end. Each one signifies God's good and perfect gift. My first divine intervention, is explained in a simple practical way.

God will never leave us or forsake us. If God be for you, who can be against you. There is nothing God won't do to help us in a transition. Nothing we go through in life can separate us from the love of God. Religion likes to make God's love conditional, but it is undoubtedly, unconditional... He cares about us. The world, flesh and the devil may try to sidetrack us and get us off the glory road into mud holes, but the Lord loves us even in the mire....help is on the way. Help may come through circumstances, people, angels, reading God's Word, or miracles. Remember, He controls the wind and the waves so we know He can do the impossible to help us.

My life began in the Alleghany Mountains, in a little village called Richburg in New York State, population 250. It had once been a boom town in the late 1800s with the discovery of oil. The town grew to 13,000 people, and printed its own currency. Everyone was rich and so was Richburg. The town gradually dwindled every year after the oil wells dried up. My great grandfather was in the midst of the boom and was very wealthy. My father was raised by his grandfather in the oil fields drilling wells. His mom and dad (my grandparents) divorced when he was a young boy, so his grandpa Putman raised him. He grew up with money and all the popularity and good times money gives. He had never been disciplined and had to have everything his way. My dad got sick in junior high and quit school to go live with his aunt in

Binghamton NY until he got better, then he returned to the oil fields with his grandfather. My mom lived in nearby Olean, a town of 13,000. It was always busy and very exciting with the main street stores of Walworths, and Sears plus many others. Santa made a visit to the town every Christmas, so that was as big as it got to me as little boy. My mother's being the oldest child of four, took on the responsibility of all the cooking and cleaning because both parents had to work, and then the her father died when she was in high school. Her mom, my grandma worked in a cutlery and as a dish washer in the Olean House Hotel. She attended a large high school and was extremely beautiful, (the pick of the prom for every guy). She loved to dance and did so every Friday night. My father also went there every Friday night where they eventually met. He was in his early 20's and she had just finished high school. He loved to dance and was the standout in the crowd. He had jet black curly hair and confidence to conquer with all that money can buy. My mom was swept off her feet with his romantic ways. They ran off and got married by the justice of the peace to begin their exciting lives in Richburg NY. Richburg had a few hillbilly's, some of which did not have a high school education. People did not know proper lexicon, nor etiquette language, but rather used adjectives and cursing. Their lives revolved around hunting and fishing. These were my dad's favorite activities. The main past time of the boys was to fight... Just beat the crap out of each other...stupid, but nonetheless true.

My first day in Kindergarten, I was in a fight within the first hour of class. You had to deal with fights just to go to the bathroom. I remember, the teachers being all old maids until I was in the sixth grade, just miserable, over weight, grumpy, middle aged ladies who did not like children. I had ADS (Attention Deficit Syndrome) so I was troubled and somehow always getting into trouble. I was a dreamer and because of lack of attention, they constantly disciplined me by throwing chalk,pulling my hair and ears, locked in closets, and shoved under teachers desks or banished to the hall. Two things saved me from total destruction at an early age, I got my mother's good looks. I remember my mother's encouraging words, that I would make it, because I was a cute little boy with my father's effective talking ability. My father's mother once told me I had diarrhea of the mouth, but it helped me at times make new friends. Girls liked me and help me of which one was the twin daughter of the principle. This most likely was the cause of the guys ganging up on me. I would get threats throughout the day that they planned to beat me up after school, so I simply stood my ground and showed no fear, and it worked. Nonetheless, I still made friends with several of my class mates that became my bodyguards. God was with me through the elementary grades to enable me to get through this stage in my life. There were two wonderful things in my life. First my mother was a beautiful angel, my dearest friends, who created another world for me in the midst of this tragic situation. She whistled all the time, and showed great love toward me with her constant smiles and big brown eyes. She went out of her way to make me special meals, and treats. Mom always made me feel important and involved me in all her tasks. She would listen for hours to my dreams and not say a negative thing about them ...making me believe my dreams would come true.

My dad however, had no time for me and would rather I not be in the same room as him. His harsh words to me consisted of: "Get out of my way, leave me alone, you are not going to amount to a hill of beans." Nonetheless, as a small child, I willingly obeyed orders to shovel snow three foot high, on sidewalks and the driveway, before he would even rise in the morning. I continued mowing his lawn, cleaned his car, and painted his house with NO recompense, ever. I had odd jobs throughout the community, that graciously were able to pay my way all through the years I lived at home.

The second thing in my life that changed everything and brought divine intervention was the little Church I grew up in. The congregation numbered less than hundred but they were kind, loving people who believe in me and raised me spiritually speaking.

They put me in the Christmas pageant when I was in the sixth grade and gave me a speaking part which I couldn't remember when the time came. I was so embarrassed, but they still encouraged me. The church was my family. I started singing in the choir when in 7th grade, and sang tenor to start, then switched to base when graduating from high school. There were church dinners once a month, and everyone had to say their favorite verse. Mine was, "We love Him because He first loved us." This became a very profound promise to me because my mother felt it would be easy for me to remember. They always involved me in the skits putting me in the front row and cheered me on.

We were and still are in battles in our lives, walking through one transition after another. There will be those who try to destroy and come against you, that seem to constantly torment without let up. But remember, "No weapon formed against us shall prosper and any tongue that rises up against us in judgment shall and will be condemned, for this is our heritage as child of the King. Isaiah 54:17. Unfortunately, many times those very people are family and friends.

My nickname which derived from home was "brubbie" and this carried over into school where they called me "grub." There was no faith in me from family, but it didn't matter because I had the Love of the prettiest woman on earth, my sweet beautiful brilliant mother who would always make me feel like a winner.

School was a zoo, music, art and sports overruled all the goof balls I went to school with. I was in the band in sixth grade, played the trombone. Band would let out at lunch time. We were in a central school one big building. High school and junior high were up stairs, grade school was on the first floor, cafeteria and band room were in the basement. The high school bigtimers would eat lunch in the band room. These egocentric boys needed to get the attention of the girls. So they abased me to impress them, by suspended me upside down in the band room. I was left hanging by the exposed water pipes from the ceiling, with kettle drums under me as they watched me dangle while they ate.

Though the experiences were trying, I still loved to play the trombone, sing in the choir and go to art classes. My parents regardless of all the negative at school, would never let me miss, but only if I had a fever. It would go to 13 below zero in the winter and because my father was too parsimonious to give me lunch money that I was forced to walk in the cold to and from to get my lunch, and many times I would make a sack lunch to avid the cold. It was like living a prison sentence growing up, with the exception of mother, church, music, art, and sports. In a town of

250 people there were only three places to go in the freezing winter: the church, the library, or school.

I loved to go to the reading time at the Colonial Library, because my aunt Etha was the librarian. It was so cozy and clean and I felt comfortable because I did not have to read out loud. This was just to listen and learn. As a young boy, I was placed in a special education class, because of my ineptness at reading. Early on, my reading disability was recognized immediately, because my dream world overruled my concentration. This special reading class caused me to feel nauseous and shaky because I was a misfit. My mother had always dressed me to look like a million dollar kid, so my appearance would veil the disability. In contrast to me, the other children in this special reading class smelled terrible, looked terrible and were generally unkempt. I recall the book we had to read out loud, and the only word I knew was my name...for the title read, "Alice and Jerry." I felt so bad, and thought I was the dumbest cluck on earth...always in trouble with the teachers because of talking to find out what page we were on. This disability coupled with my dad's put down made me feel fearful and worthless.

One day at the meal table my dad said, "Brub, see that power house out there...(a shed that was used by the oil men who worked the wells in the back hills)... you can live there when you grow up." That comment stayed me through out my younger years as I grew up looking at that shed and trying to plan my life as a little boy. Thinking perhaps, if I could get a chicken, I would have a friend that laid eggs. Then I could eat them as fried, sunny side, hard boiled or scrambled. I could grow a garden and have a cow and I would make it. This was a passage I had to get through in my thinking in order to plan my future, knowing my father would most likely never help me. My dear precious Mom in order to please my father, fed us on .50 cent meals and my father would hunt a deer and feed us venison for months. This caused me to start gathering pop bottles from the dump and around town so I could buy candy bars, ice cream and soda. This gave me the energy I was lacking from constantly eating canned foods. The end result made me very thin and hyper.

Being so hyper, I could not sleep and rocked in my bed every night. This upset my parents and I would awake while 'sleep rocking', to my mom or dad paddling me to wake up and stop rocking. In attempt to stop this, I would go in and sleep on the foot of my sisters bed every night. She had the front room of the house with the large windows. It was a wonderful place to go and fall asleep, but, of course I would have to get to my bed before deep sleep came, in order to avoid getting caught in my sister's room. I hoped I could become smart like her by laying on the end of her bed because everything was so easy for her.

We took a bath only once a week, on Saturday night. They would fill the tube and we all took our turns taking a bath. Without question, I slept well on Saturday night's with no rocking, because of bathing and resting on clean sheets. I awoke Sunday morning feeling like a million bucks. I was taken to Sunday school by my aunt, but I didn't like to go because they made us read out loud which as I mentioned earlier was very nerve wracking for me. However the worship in church was very enjoyable and soon this song became my comfort that carried me through... IN MY HEART THERE RINGS A MELODY. God spoke to me through this precious song in a supernatural way, assuring me I was not alone. He was there with me and everything would be ok . Somehow I would amount to something.

I got through the third, fourth, and fifth grades by going to my teacher's and telling them how much I appreciated them and how I promised to work hard and be a much better student if they did NOT hold me back. They listened and said they would pass me on probation if I studied hard throughout the summer with the books they would give me, and to become a better student with higher grades the next year. However, my mother grew frustrated on the first reading every summer, and that became my first and last. She was such a sweet loving person, but when it came to my then insufficiency to read, she had no patience to handle it. I recall one teacher saying

DIVINE INTERVENTION: CONFESSIONS OF A PASTOR

that I made it by the skin of my teeth. Afterwards I remember looking in the mirror for the supposed sink on my teeth.

My older sister was a perfect straight A student. At report card time Dad would be super dramatic after the evening meal, and read my sisters straight A card first. Then mine, and with the same histrionics, dad would degrade me as he read my report card out loud. Mom got so nervous and she came to my defense, reminding my dad that I was not as gifted in that area as my sister. And I agreed with mom to calm dad down.

Chapter 2

SUDDEN &ABUNDANT FAVOR

9am

Brisk School Day

A Neighboring Miracle

Jeremiah 29:11 For I know the plans I have for you," declares the LORD, "plans to prosper you and not to harm you, plans to give you hope and a future.

I'm not a religious nor a political minded person... I'm a people person. But I grew up in extreme religious Pharisee minded atmosphere. My church would not allow us to dance, go to movies, or play cards. In trying to keep these rules along with my learning disability I was very unhappy with my life.

But I experienced Divine Intervention in the 5th grade at the bottom of what seemed to be a place of no hope. A creative traveling evangelist came for a week of meetings at our little church. He was a musician and used magic in his preaching as well as in his personal conversations with young people. He pulled a silver dollar out of my hair which got my attention. He was staying in one of the church people's homes while in town. So, I went to say hi every day. He was always so kind and spent time showing me how he did his tricks. He was a very sharp dresser and drove a Pontiac convertible. When he asked me to go with him to another church on Wednesday night where he was the guest speaker, I proudly accepted. That night after his message he asked who wanted to accept Jesus into their lives and I went forward in front of a church of strangers and prayed with someone. And they read to me **I John 5: 1112. And this is the testimony God has given us eternal life, and this life is in His Son. He who has the Son has life; he who does Not have the Son of God, does not have life. I write these things to you, who believe in the name of the Son of God, so that you may know that you have eternal life.**

That night I drove a stake in the ground to remember these verses.

God met me there in that little church, that night, which was surely a divine appointment. From that day on I knew I had a Heavenly Father who watched over me, who will take me to heaven to be with Him someday. Since then I knew I have never been alone.

After this real salvation experience, my schooling took a turn for the better. My entrance into the sixth grade was probationary. The teacher was one of the meanest in school. She had a mental breakdown and was replaced by Mrs. Murdock who lived across the street from me with her husband Don and daughter Nan. This new teacher, knew who I was and what had to be done for me in order to enhance my future. She was aware I couldn't follow or read out loud, so she told me to sit quietly during the oral reading times and much to my relief, I never had to read aloud again. This amazing teacher was sent by God to help me through these years. The Lord used her to favor me above the rest. My artistic ability was what she chose to use to nurture my confidence to where it should be. Numerous times she asked me to take care of the room decorations by changing them constantly with the seasons and holidays. Then she gave me the project to use my artistic talent to decorate the main halls and entrances of the entire school, hence showing all the children (particularly the bullies), and facility, that I was someone special. Everyone saw my work and this Godsent teacher also put me on the honor roll list, for all students and parents to view.

Chapter 3

THE VALUE OF FORGIVENESS
THAT FOLLOWS GRIEF

8pm

Christmas Eve

Back hills of New York

Psalm 89:1 I will sing of the LORD's great love forever; with my mouth I will make your faithfulness known through all generations.

There was a neighboring town called Bolivar, one mile from ours, a town of 2000. A special occasion came when we were to ride on the sixth graders bus to Buffalo for the Shrine Circus. I was so excited, my mom gave me 25 cents. I got on the bus and everyone wanted to know how much money each person had. They all had ten dollars and I was embarrassed to say I only had a quarter. They all looked at me as the poorest person in the world. Well at the circus they all look out for me and bought me whatever everyone else was buying to eat throughout the circus. I realized from that experience that my family was not going to look out for me, or help me in my future... so I determined to work from then on and save every cent I had to go to college and buy a house and car, which all seemed so far off and somewhat impossibility at the time, but God put sheer determination in my heart to do so.

There was an elderly lady who had two beagle dogs that need to be walked every day. Mrs. Burtsole, Henry and Carrie. I went and asked for the job, and got it, for 10 cents a day, 70 cents a week, two dollars and eighty cents a month. As time went on I became a good friend to her... her husband had died which had happened to be one of the richest men in Richburg. She had a son who was an alcoholic that I got to know as well. Gerald liked me so much he decided he wanted me to work with him to landscape the yard that was over grown and unkept. This would be every day, all day, for a week . He said he would pay me 50 cents an hour. When we began, he was on the wagon for the week sober as a church mouse. He said to begin, "Remember Rome wasn't built in a day, but rather brick by brick." So we worked with a careful plan he had drawn out and took short breaks in the morning for cookies, lunch and a break in the afternoon . I was having a great time and getting paid for it. We completed everything at the end of the week. It was the best looking lawn in town and I had learned how to do landscaping. I had made twenty dollars in a weeks' time and was not use to seeing such money. He then said I was hired to be their weekly landscaper. So then I had two jobs each week. Walking the dogs and landscaping their yard. I was so pleased as a growing young man to earn money the right way and be appreciated and compensated for it. I proudly and carefully saved my six dollars and eighty cents a month.

I realized the best money that could be made in the town for a young person would be to get a paper route. The Buffalo Breeze was a Saturday and Sunday paper so that paper route would not be the best pay. The Olean Times Herald, however, was Monday through Friday and that was the job I wanted. Eventually I found the boy who had the route and asked if I could peddle his route with him every night until he was ready to give it to me. He agreed so I peddled papers every night with him for a year. Got to know him and his family real well and had dinner with them many times after finishing the route. I was making $ 8.80 a month and saving every penny. Well the day came that he gave the route to me. I was just starting the 7th grade. Immediately I realized I could increase my earnings by getting more customers and also be recognized by the paper company who could possibly give me free trips and reward money. So I extended my route to every place I could ride my bike. I was then making twenty five dollars a month from the route. I helped my sister make money too, by allowing her to peddle papers and clean my lawn mower and paid her to do it. Combined I earned my money by mowing lawns and the paper route.

However, school had its ups and downs and in certain areas it continued to be a challenge. I was passed to the 7th grade and my sixth grade teacher realized there were two trouble makers in the class who had been there since kindergarten. She held one of them back and let the other go on to seventh grade. He went from my #1 enemy when he hung with the other kid to becoming a good friend. One of the things that brought us close was survival in the Zoo. We were now on the 2nd floor with the junior high, but so was the high school students and some were major trouble makers. They came around at the end of lunch and stood in the island of the stair well, waiting for those coming from the cafeteria. As they passed through, they would grab us separately and begin shoving us back and forth in their circle, while calling us every name they could think of. This of course, got the attention from the top and bottom floor students as well. It was total humiliation every day. One night I was walking on the main street of Richburg heading home and a car pulled alongside me. It was D. Sisson and Larry B. they were the meanest most feared boys in the school. I was in the seventh grade along with Larry and Dean. The school held back those who did not want to work to graduate in the seventh grade. They were 15 and would be leaving school at years end. But I chose to befriend those tough guys in class because I needed some bodyguards. Dean and Larry were not only two of the tough guys but they were my bodyguard friends. They told me to get into the car. I did, we were buds. They said we were all going up into the hills to take on the Ward boys. I asked how many were there, and they said, '7'. "But there is just three of us," I shouted. Then they explained their strategy. They said we could walk up to the 7 of them, stand and talk for a minute, then turn to walk away, but instead with backs turned make a fist with both of your hands and swing around, giving three of them an upper cut. Then there would be only four left and we could handle them. I agreed, and we drove to the hills. These are my buds, so I'm prepared to help them, but I was also shaking inside thinking if we go to the hills and get killed, my parents would have no idea where I was, and who would find us? Well, we drove up to the Ward house where one of the boys was outside and I asked if he and his brothers wanted to see us. He was scared silly and said, no, no one wants to see you." So there was no fight, and I became a sworn friend. Driving back off the hill, I mentioned to Dean and Larry about the junior and senior boys that had been standing by the cafeteria hall, waiting for me and others to put in their circle of torment on the way out. I asked them if they could possibly do something about it.

They said, "no problem, tell them to meet you in the boys locker room and we'll go with you and take care of them." So I let it be known to have the ring leader of the bad boys whose name was also Larry, meet me in the locker room the next morning before class. I gathered all my fighting buddies including Roy and waited in the locker room.... Knowing the ones coming in after us, were eager to beat the crap out of me. There was 7 of us, and eight of them. Now, I was shaking at my knees.... Being 6 ft. tall but a weed in the wind. As Larry and Dean came around the corner, the looks on their faces changed dramatically. They went from cocky to concerned. One of them asked if we were all together, and when Larry and Dean said, "yea, you want to do something about it?" They wimped out, said no, and shuffled quickly out of there. I never had to encounter that humiliating cafeteria circle experience again. Those trouble makers had left me alone. Thank God, HE intervenes even in our youthful concerns.

The teacher for the seventh grade was Mr. Max who handled himself perfectly, with total professionalism at all times . He wanted absolute respect and also gave it. He was my first male teacher, and what a great example to follow. I was excited about school for the first time because I was 6 ft. tall, and was asked to play on the junior high basketball team by the school coach. It was a natural for me+ and I scored 7 points and blocked 10 shots my first game.

I also started going to Youth For Christ rallies once a month on Saturday nights, then to the club in the school. They challenged us to carry our Bibles to class, so I always did. Soon I began making more friends, but somehow I was never invited to their Friday night wild parties that the junior high had. Even though I wanted to be invited, I believe God stopped me from getting involved with the wrong crowd and kept me clean. So I kept myself busy with a new found project... a 49 Plymouth. The Shawmut Railroad Track was on the back of our property. It was shut down when I was 5. After the tracks were pulled up it became a road. Because it was on the outskirts of town, we didn't need the necessary legalities to use the old rail road track run. My dad (who rarely showed me kindness and concern), actually cared to tell me about an old rusted out '49 Plymouth. The price was a good deal for $75.00... so I bought it thinking I would fix it up and drive it someday. I worked on this car for four years. Eventually I found a buddy in town who knew everything about cars. He helped me with the mechanics, replaced the starter, the driveshaft, the transmission, put a radio in, changed the tail lights and put 1953 Cadillac conversions and backup lights. It was beginning to look like one fancy ride. I sanded the body down, filled all the rust spots with plastic body filler, and cleaned a neighbors old horse stable to paint it. I recall us using a fly spray can, and hand pumping the sprayed paint. It took a week. I put white sidewalls on it, chrome moon disk hubcaps on the front, and fender skirts on the back. It was some good looking car. I carefully drove my car keeping it in good shape. Other guys got cars and put them on the tracks. Bill Hermen said his horse could beat my friends 37 Chevy in a quarter mile race on the track. So we marked it out. The town came to see it. I road with my friend Jack in the race as it was his car. The horse was way in the lead as we began but then Jack put his car into third gear and we flew by the horse, past the finish line, and parked the car across the tracks. But none of us knew that it would take a while to stop the horse from running. So the horse came at our car at full gallop. Bill, who was on its back, had to jump the horse over the hood of Jacks car while we sat inside speechless. Thank God no one was hurt, in our country way of living.

Well the '49 Plymouth was my joy and when the time came for me to drive it on the road to school and on dates, It brought me to new experiences and cross roads in my life. Though I had been driving my car on the back roads, it had yet to be insured. But, dad said he wouldn't pay for the insurance and if I used my money, I wouldn't be able to go to college. All my friends were driving and went on dates. I walked and if I took a girl on a date, my dad drove us... which wasn't cool at all, so I didn't date. This changed how I was seen in the school till my graduation. So junior high was a positive period in so many ways. Church, school, sports, and work consumed by little world.

We had a log cabin on Rushford Lake where we spent our summer weekends. With the money from my paper route, I bought a 7 horse motor from Ray in my church for 75.00. Then found an old sunk boat in the lake and repaired it throughout the winter months. That spring I had a nice free refurbished motor boat to run around the lake on. It would go 17 miles an hour and easily blended in with the other boats. We also had a blackberry patch in the hills in Richburg. For a little extra money and to keep me busy, I picked wild blackberries every summer and would sell them from my boat at the lake for 25 cents a basket. It was a lot of fun and I continued to save money for college.

It would be wrong if I did not pen the realness of our lifestyle as a "wealthy" family. We were wealthy to an extent that we had a vacation cottage on the lake, a boat, and lived in a very nice neighborhood. You could say, that I was a "protected" child with privileges that most others at my school did not have, which was the number one reason the bad boys picked on me. Jealousy runs deep even in the backwoods. But to compare our wealth with the wealth of orange county, CA would not be a fair evaluation. As I had mentioned before, my dad was raised with as much money as he desired. But along with that came a penurious spirit and selfishness, which he carried over into his small family of four. We had plenty of money, but dad refused to share it with any of us unless necessary. My mother did her best to dress me well, but with no money to spend, it became embarrassing the older I got. These side jobs I have been writing about paid my way as I grew from a boy to a man. Though it was hard, it taught me how to earn my own way, and with the grace of God guiding my paths, the Lord has blessed me abundantly beyond all my dreams. What the devil had intended for my bad, GOD turned for my good.

During these discovering years in my youth, I had learned to adjust to my dad's coldness and resentment. I had hoped throughout the years that as I accomplished things, he would recognize my potential and at least comment. But those words would not be heard for years to come. My mother, did her best to fill in, as she knew I was dis turbed by his character. When there is a parental void in anyone's life, GOD will always send many substitutes to sooth the edges. In this case, one of those people was a neighbor named Bob who worked with me on general fundamentals . He was an older man that was employed at the bank in Bolivar. The real joy of my life at that time was my little dog Corky, which I had grown to love deeply since the sixth grade. It was his birthday on Christmas. That evening Corky had followed my dad out on the back walk to my grandmother's house. My dad did not look back to see if Corky had followed him, and our dog ran into the street. Bob, our neighbor and his friend were driving by the house on the snowy road clipping along pretty fast, when Corky ran in front of them. They hit him and immediately, Corky made his way to the closest pine tree and died. I still feel emotion when I talk about it. We went out and found him and picked his limp body up from under the tree. I couldn't believe he was gone. It seemed like grief greater than I could bare at such a young age. This was not a problem I could fix. I never thought I would be able to get over it, but later learned that time truly heals inner pain and grief. Of course I hated Bob and his friend Jack who ran over Corky. In order to make amends with me, the next summer Bob asked me if I would be interested in learning the fundamentals of playing basketball. I hesitated, but because of my love for basketball, I agreed. He had a basket on his barn door which each night we practiced on. Through this sensitive season, I began to forgive him and became a good basketball player. This carried over into the school year where my coach saw my potential and helped develop me. Had I not forgiven Bob for ending the life of my dearest companion which I loved so much, that hatred would have built in my heart only to increase over time, and result in a life of anger. Thank God, HE used the tool of basketball to help me realize the value of forgiveness following grief.

As a prerequisite to play basketball, I first had to join the soccer team, which was made up of freshman through seniors. I soon found out that the older boys had it in for me, because I was good enough to play as a freshman on a mostly older team. Riding home on a school bus from an away game, two juniors in the seat behind me took their steel chin guards which were covered with foam rubber and whacked me over the head. Then they took their sweaty long sleeved shirts off and tied the sleeves into knots for a second assault. I was getting a little jumpy with this after a while. I thought I was getting killed. SO I decided to defend myself with my chin guards and return their fire. I hit the meanest, most feared senior in the school right over the head. Immediately, the guys jumped out of their seats and pulled my shirt off, stretched me over the seats and slapped my belly till it turned pink. Finally the coach who was on the bus stopped this, which he should have initially done... remember these guys are hillbilly, so this was totally acceptable behavior. When we arrived back at the locker room, with the coach nowhere in sight to keep these guys in check, they put me in the shower with all my clothes on...and in the freezing winter weather, that was how I had to walk home. It was a cultural understanding that this was good for me. Dad never expressed concern in this type of thing but rather wanted to see me tough it out. Well praise God, I didn't become an out of control tough ruffian, getting in bar brawls', or lashingout with anger at innocent folks, like the hoodlums I had to put up with.

The summer after the eighth grade I realized there was another way to make money in the village... cut grass. Now to do this I had to have a lawn mower, and a way to transport it each place. Dad financed me to buy a nice lawnmower, the best, for $ 75.00 and pay him back as I found jobs. Shortly thereafter, I met with the fellow who had cornered the market on all the yards in town. I offered, Gary my free services to assist him with each lawn, if he would give me his business after that summer, because he was going into his senior year. He agreed and the next summer I had all his lawns as well as the town cemetery which was a real plum back then, of $25.00 for each mowing. Then I realized that digging graves paid twenty five dollars a piece. The next day II asked the cemetery committee if I could start digging graves and would show them an example of my work, and they agreed. After they laid out the measurements, I began to dig. Immediately, I began to dig a hole of 6 ft. down. Each foot I had to throw the dirt up higher out of the hole. By dinner time I had only dug 4 ft. down. Taking a break, I went home for dinner and told dad and mom that I was not going to make it. I was exhausted, had two feet yet to go, and the sun was going down. With his typical characteristic hardnosed manner, my dad told me to go finish digging and not come back until it was done, adding that he did not care if it took me all night. So, I dug into the night, still had a foot to go down in between valets...working in pitch dark, it became very unnerving. Thinking I would never get out of there, I heard my dad's voice and to his credit, and very much unlike his nature, I heard him holler for me to get out of there. Much to my surprise, he jumped down in the hole and what seemed like minutes, my dad finished the job and we went home. Well of course I realized from that experience, I would never start something I was not sure I could finish.

Chapter 4

HUMILIATION TO HONOR...
DEGRADATION TO DESTINY

6 p.m

Award Ceremony

Top of Class

Psalm 71:1 In You oh Lord I have taken refuge that I may never be put to shame.

My freshmen year I had to face a major cross roads in my life. Geometry, is was a state required class that had to be passed to graduate. Unfortunately it is memorizing 28 theorems plus knowing when and how to apply them to a mathematical problem, which I was unable to do. At the end of the school year I had a 49 gpa in the class. My high school education, and all my dreams were seemingly coming to an abrupt end. Moreover, the teacher Ms. Flanagan didn't like me, since I was making her look bad. New York State has a regents' exam for every required course which was taken along with the school exam... and in fact over ruled the school exam. If you could pass it, it didn't matter what you did in class because you passed the course. I went up to my study room the night before the state exam, and chose three theorems, memorized them and prayed they would be on the test. The next day, when I opened the test, there they were. When Ms. Flanagan gave me my grade she expressed amazement that I had passed geometry. This meant I would continue to the sophomore class. I knew then that Almighty God came out of heaven to help me in the destiny of my life.

I had my off road car, my boat, and was no longer an underclassman in high school but a sophomore and everything was wonderful. We had a great soccer season and went to the play offs. JV basketball was awesome, and our team had the best record in the league. I was doing good in all subjects in school, and had saved a lot for college with the gardening business in the summer, but had given up the paper route to play sports. I was in the high school choir, traversing with them to county events, as well as in sports. I went to school on February 19th, which was my 16th birthday, and sat next to John Cooper, in choir and that day he said ominously to me, "we are going to get you today," which put fear in my bones. I knew they put people through the paddle wheel in basketball practice... when one crawls through the legs of the 24 Junior varsity and varsity, they swat your behind as you pass through. But that wasn't what was planned for me that night after practice. The coach's had agreed to allow the guys to hold me down and paddle my bare behind 16 times from each of 24 guys. I did not know for sure why this happened but it is safe to conclude that it must have been a statement against my witness, because I was a bold Christian. There was no one on the team who shared my faith. Because of my vision of going to college I was able to dismiss the entire incident.... and though my behind was hurting, I was not intimidated or deterred to miss practice the next day. It was pleasing to me to show these cretinous louts that I was above their antics and had higher aspirations than they. I just stayed focused on my goals and my love of basketball and we had the # 2 finish in the JV league. At the end of the season I was asked to join the varsity team and we won the league championship for the first time in 28 yrs. The school year book was dedicated to our team with our pictures in the front. What Satan meant to harm me with, God used to bless me. I continued to play for the next 2 yrs. and made the County all Star team my senior year.

My junior year I was popular because of the championship in basketball the previous season. I was finally invited to a school party which I had always wanted to go to since junior high. Much to my chagrin, it was a drunken make out fest. Somehow I ended up sitting on a couch with a cheerleader in the dark, and began feeling very uncomfortable. This was an ungodly atmosphere, and did not hold a candle to what I had been experiencing in church...so I quickly excused myself as I pulled the cheerleader off my lap. That experience was a turning point in my life... a watershed regarding those parties I had longed to attend. I knew I needed something to find my direction for the years ahead. So, I decided to increase my church attendance by going to Wednesday night prayer meetings. Weekly, I would sit in the back by the pot belly stove with the old folks and harry butler, a deacon in the church. No young people were there and half the time was spent on our knees praying as I heard these people cry out to God for direction. I began to get comfortable and pray along with them. This gave me a peace to deal with life.

I was in the junior class play and selected by the teachers to go to boys state that summer at Colgate University. I arrived in the dorm and was talking to the guys on my floor and realized I needed to excuse myself to go to the men's room. I was in such a hurry to get there I ran down the hall. A boy stopped me on the way and said I was speeding on a city street and immediately wrote me a ticket. I went back to the guys I had been talking to and told them what had just happened. One of them said he wanted to be my lawyer and defend me in court. The next morning everyone in the dorm attended my trial as my Lawyer pleaded temporary insanity and I was ruled innocent. Next the guys came to me and said I was the most wellknown person in the city and they wanted me to run for a senate position in the state (which was a metaphor for student counsel in the college). I ran, and won. I was the first person from my country to win a senate position at Boys State College.

In that same year prior to going to Boy's State, my cousin David, asked me to go with him on Friday and Saturday nights and carry his Hammond organ, I agreed. We were asked to bring his organ to a Friday night youth rally where I heard about their summer High School camp. I filled out an application for employment at the camp, and immediately was accepted. After Boy's State I went to Word of Life to work. My initial job there was to transport people across the lake to the Island where the high school camp was. It was an amazing summer with 500 high school kids coming to the Island each week and we had to transport them by boat. It was a divine breakthrough in my life because my dad didn't let me drive his boat or his car. I was driving boats that were the most expensive boats available. We had a barge that held 50 people and three 13 passenger boats as well as three water ski boats. I loved it, and the staff were all college students from Christian Schools. In fact I fell in love with one of the ladies named Karen, a sophomore at this University... I chased after her all summer. On a day off one evening, I took her by the lake and tried to give her my school ring. I dropped it in the grass and we spent a long time trying to find it. After we did she turned me down. But my relationship with her caused me to look at this Christian University that I would attend.

There were so many challenging things that happened in working 8am till 11pm with all the activities of the boats. Each afternoon I was to go over to the mainland where the Inn was. I taught the adults how to water ski and pulled all who wanted to do so. It was the last day of the camp as I continued to do my job. I got in the boat to start out for the main dock to pick up the lifeguard who rode with me. I had just gotten a little way from the dock when the motor stalled. Upon examination of the motor I saw that the ski rope was tangled in the propeller. I jumped in the water, and untangled the rope. Still in the water I turned the motor toward me to start it by the handpull, because the battery was dead. The motor started immediately, and I realized to my horror that the boat was in gear and the throttle was wide open. The boat sped away off into the lake. I realized there could be a terrible accident and I would go to jail. As we all watched, I saw that because I had turned the motor to start it, the boat began spinning in a big circle and passing by the beach in front of me each time. I also saw that it was getting closer to the shore with each passing. In time it would have run through the main dock where the lifeguard was watching it. I decided I didn't want to go to jail so if I treaded water in the path of the craft, I could grab ahold of its side and clamber up into the boat. As the boat approached I did exactly that and by the miracle of an angel helping me, I caught the boat and got aboard. In relief, I went and picked up the lifeguard and drove to the dock... and calmly asked who wanted to ski first. Everyone stood dumb founded staring at me. This certainly was one of many times there would be divine intervention in my life. The next day I went to the mainland to turn the keys into the office. As I crossed the road to the inn a car passed with too young men in it who looked at me and said something and I waved at them. They stopped their car just up the road by the cliffs overlooking the lake shore. They signaled for me to come and talk so I did when I got up to them they grabbed me and said I had given them the finger. I disagreed. But one of them took me to the edge of the cliff and was raising his hand to hit me in the face and knock me over the cliff. The other guy grabbed his arm as it was in the air and said, "I believe him, he seems to me a good person." The anger left them both and they wanted to know who I was. Somewhat relieved, I told them about our camp meeting (which was taking place that night), and invited them to come. They shook my hand and drove off. Just then a group of guys who saw the whole thing ran up to save me. Again divine intervention.

My senior year was one of the happiest times of my life. My dad had mellowed out enough to give me his jeep to drive and then his car. My dad paid for my school lunches (first time ever), paid for my hair to be cut at the local barber shop (rather than my mother cutting it), and he bought my new clothes for school. What a pleasant feeling to know my dad seemed to show value in me after my return from Word of Life Camp. I was the president of my class, captain of the soccer team, had the lead role for the senior play, and captain of the basketball team. I went to the state track finals in 440 as the captain. I also spoke at the American Legion meetings about how I was a senator and the basic government of Boys State College. They were the ones whom had sponsored me to go to Boys State. I wrote to Karen at this Christian University and applied to go there and was accepted to be in the class of 62.

My class took a senior trip to Washington DC, I played in the band, sang in the State Choir and the All County Choir. In addition I graduated with the American Legion Award, Industrial Arts Award, History Award, Dick Jennings Leadership Award, a scholarship award from my church for college and another scholarship award from a person in the church. Both scholarships continued through 7 years of school, and my sister and her husband gave me their tithe for 7 years. The village hired me to paint the town library the summer before college began. As I went to this southern

University, my first year I saved $1000.00 which was the exact amount for room, board and tuition.

It is obvious that up to this point in my life Divine Intervention was constant. The mercies of God that are new and fresh every day. The love of God which is for all. The earth is the Lord's and everything in it. We live move and breath in Him. We experience just a little glimpse of heaven on this earth through nature's beauty and through God's presence. Hell is simply going into eternity without God. So for someone, God forbid this is as close to heaven as they will ever get. At some point every person has to make a decision, the most important decision, is Jesus the Son of God? yes or no? Yes, and you are heaven bound because it's not by works of righteousness that we have done but according to his mercy He saved us. I want to say for everyone right now, Lord have mercy. Bring us to a right decision daily. Now God is going to be involved in your life, whether you believe in Him or not, or in heaven or hell. He cares about everyone. But Satan is the prince of the power of the air and wants to deceive, steal and destroy. He and his cohorts are on a mission of destruction. The constant murders on the earth are all from him. This is when we pray, "Lord have mercy for divine intervention and divine appointments".

Perhaps this analogy will help. I found an ice cream store that gives away free ice cream, and I want to give you the address. Most of us scream for icecream, it's one of the joys of life. Well the God who made icecream has also made a heaven for all of us. Just put your hand in the hand of the man who stills the waters and calmed the sea. Simple, Simple, Simple, I believe, I believe, I believe. God wants to put us through faith in Jesus on the fast track of life. **Anticipation= expect a miracle, participation= get a miracle, acceleration= know constant miracles, intensification= see that nothing is impossible with God**. Jeremiah knew this: He said "Ah Lord God you have made the heavens and the earth with your own out stretched hand, Nothing is impossible with you." So we go into faith mode expecting miracles , speaking miracles in our conversations. Seeing miracles in our lives.

Chapter 5

GOD CAN REDEEM OUR EVERY DECISION

1pm

Dating Hall

University

Matthew 7:78 "Ask and it will be given to you; seek and you will find; knock and the door will be opened to you. For everyone who asks receives; the one who seeks finds; and to the one who knocks, the door will be opened.

Life is full of transitions and change. I went to a strict Christian university in the south. I am a country boy from a village in the Allegany mountains of 250 people and I went to South Carolina to a University of 3000 plus a High School academy and a graduate school.

This amazing university was the place God used to help me overcome the first level of my learning disability.

Yes, only by God's grace I was able to enter a high end university without having the same educational level as the others in the college. God allowed teacher after teacher to grace me through each grade and then each class in college to achieve a high B upon graduation. In order to keep my retention level, I made notes of key information on subjects in classes that I knew I could be quizzed on without notice. Even though it may have appeared unattractive, I walked around with huge wrist rings which held my 5X8 note cards. Seeing the note cards constantly, helped me pass all my quizzes and tests. Truly this university played a great part not only in my spiritual life, but my educational career. 34/

It was quite an a period of adjustment for me. I recall walking on campus one day in all black, with the exception of white socks. Attending the school auditorium that afternoon, I thought I looking pretty sharp in a black blazer, pants, shirt and shoes and didn't think much of my beaming white socks until my roommates had a fashion talk with me that night.

Of course I listened and learned from their fashion advice, but my focus was two things; working to pay my way through four years of college and getting off probation after the first semester, in order to stay in school. God put the "super" to my "natural" by providing the money for me to attend college and seminary. Not only did my sister help me financially, but the church also gave me $25.00 each month for seven years. Another couple sent me $5.00 each month for seven years which between all three came to $100.00 each month. God always paid the bills through one means or another for those seven years. Phil 4:19 "My God shall supply all our needs according to HIS riches in glory through Christ Jesus"!

The History of Civilization was one of the courses my first semester. We sat in an auditorium that seated 800 and listened to lectures and had pop quizzes. I was flunking every quiz. Sitting at an assigned table for meals, I constantly drew attention because I loved to talk. But after a while I be came quiet because I realized if my grade in that History class did not go up, I would be kicked out of there. The host, who sat at my lunch table asked me one day, why I was so quiet and was there something wrong? I said out loud, "I'm flunking out of School in History of Civilization Class!" Immediately, he told me not to worry and to meet him in his office on Saturday morning.

We met that Saturday morning and he explained how to study and prepare for quizzes and exams. Ultimately, I passed History of Civilization and was taken off probation and able to pursue and get my BA. My life was involved with studies , sports, and Christian service.

I loved to play basketball, and our team went from the bottom to the top in the league in the four years I was there. Many times I also went out on the weekends to Spartanburg Military Base where we would work at a coffee house for service men. We would go into the streets give the soldiers invitations to come to our coffee house for free donuts and coffee and then share the good news of Jesus Christ with them.

I was on the street one day and two gang members walked up to me and one drew a knife and pointed it at my stomach and asked me what would happen if he stabbed and killed me right there? I calmly replied that I would go to be with Jesus Christ in heaven for all eternity. He never said another word, put the knife away and walked off. I would go to Clemson University some weekends and share the gospel around the campus and in the dorms, and some prayed with us to ask Him to be their personal savior.

The most unique thing about this university was its many rules. You couldn't talk to girls before 9am or after 6pm and you had to be walking with them to your classes. All seats were assigned at meals, and classes. You could only be off campus so many hours a week. Girls had to be with chaperones. You could only date girls on campus at church, vespers or concert series. We could walk the girls to their dorms after dinner in a dating line that went for miles. You couldn't touch a girl, hold hands, or kiss them. There was a 6 inch rule for distance between couples. To date a girl you had to use the student mail system, which meant you had to write her a letter send it to her room and she could reply the same. It was pretty easy to ask a girl for a date and I dated as many as I could (if you could even call them dates). There was a dating parlor which could be used Saturdays and Sundays between church services. A freshmen could spend 2 hours a week there, a senior had unlimited time. It was like a huge furniture store...sit and talk and stare at each other. All the rules of this university seemed strange at first and then normal.

By my junior year I was made VP of my fraternity, and then VP of the Boy's Group which consisted of 700+ guys who met for Sunday School once a week. Soon, I became President of the Boy's Group, which was unheard of as a student not studying to be a minister. It was my fun, joking personality I guess that won me the Presidential position. People needed to laugh in such a stilted, regimented place, and God gave me the gift to help lighten things up.

My junior year I stopped dating all the girls except for one, who was a freshman from California. This girl took a great deal of my attention. We all went home for Christmas vacation and many of us found carpools, to share the cost of driving across the country. I drove to New York and my girlfriend went to California. I actually arranged for her to ride with one of my roommates. For their return back to South Carolina from California, my friend's father bought an old hearse, and since it was the 60's, they drove back in it. My roommate told me that my girlfriend became infatuated with one of the guys in the car on the ride back in the hearse. I broke up with the girl, but went back with her months later.

This girl was a pastors daughter, and not only was she attractive, but a talented piano player and straight A student. Every dating rule we had at the school, we chose to break.

One of those rules was you could not hold hands, so in concert and church, I would reach under my arm and hold her fingers. There were Artist series that we attended, and intermittently there were blackouts, in which we would quickly kiss. All of this was illegal per school rules, and I broke them, even though I was to set an example, being in charge of three rooms with 12 guys. The only time you could walk and talk with a girl was after 6pm was in a dating line to their dormitories. This was the highlight of the day. As a prayer captain, I skipped one meeting in order to walk in the dating line with her (Pat).

Soon after I began breaking the rules with her, a boy in my room got in trouble with a teacher, and I was called in by the Dean and asked about him. The Dean wanted to know how many times this guy prayed a week (out loud in our group prayer meeting). I recall telling him once. The Dean then yelled back at me that he told all of us to report anyone who did not pray three times. Then he scolded me with the question of why I failed to report that young man. I had to make a flash decision, and make up an excuse so he would not know that I had skipped the meeting... I said, "I thought I could handle it by myself." The Dean got up, and walked over to his door, and closed it, then stood in front of me like an old time drill sergeant, and said, "We are shipping you out tomorrow because we don't tolerate this type of attitude." Their terminology for shipping meant kicking me out of the college in my junior year.

So, I asked for mercy and the Dean gave it to me. But after this encounter, my nerves were shot, realizing the extremes of this school that affected me, as I was simply trying to get an education.

I was enamored with this girlfriend who was smart and headstrong. I fell in love with her and wanted her to be my wife. I can not speak for her, but looking back, I think she wanted to follow her family tradition and marry a pastor. Both of us were young and neither of us completely knew what we were doing yet in our lives. But we chose each other and that was it.

At this university, I decided to be a camp director because I did not like what I saw in the ministers there. Unfortunately, many I observed seemed to put themselves in a position of being above people and different in general. So becoming a pastor was the last thing on my mind. But my girlfriend saw my leadership skills, and I think wanted me to be a pastor like her father.

When I graduated I chose to go to Seminary in San Francisco where my girlfriends father was a board member. We lived separately but it was natural that we wanted to be together any chance we had. Her parents strongly believed that us living near each other in San Francisco would cause further temptation in our lives that would lead us to make mistakes, so they convinced us to get married as soon as possible, at Christmas vacation. We were married by her father in his church in my first year of seminary. I shook throughout the entire ceremony. Although I loved her, I don't think I was ready then for the demands of pastoring a church and having a wife, and I made many mistakes as a husband. However, what the devil intended for bad, the Lord God again intervenes and turns it for good! (Gen 50:20)

I believe now that God had desired for me to work with and for HIM as a pastor, and had my first wife not encouraged me to be a pastor, like her father, I may have lived a selfish life, only choosing to please myself. She and her family were dedicated and determined to help me become a minister. They saw things in me that I did not see, and without their being in my life, I would never have become a minister. For their continual encouragement I will always be grateful. God will give us gifts, and send us people, or take us to places... but if we take the situations too far instead of step by step under HIS GPS, it can harm us for life... For YOUR WORD oh LORD is a lamp unto my feet and a light unto my path.

Chapter 6

YOUTH MADE PARENTS PROUD

7pm

YOUTH RALLY

Standing Room Only

Psalm 91:12 Whoever dwells in the shelter of the Most High will rest in the shadow of the Almighty. I will say of the LORD, "He is my refuge and my fortress, my God, in whom I trust."

Thank God for Mercy beyond all my sins, and for people who have come into my life which makes it worth living. There are times of torment, weeping, despair, and seeming dead ends... but taking one day and moment at a time, gives the Lord an opportunity to help make a way where there seems to be no way. Isaiah 40:31 "But those who wait on the LORD Shall renew their strength; They shall mount up with wings like eagles, They shall run and not be weary, They shall walk and not faint". HE heals the broken heart and restores what was lost, turning despair into joy and praise. This concept carried over into my failing marriage. I truly was love struck for my wife Pat. We did everything we could for each other...but one thing after another caused major stress in my schooling and finances, which led to our marriage turning sour little by little. We were in ministry throughout our entire relationship from beginning to end, with its heavy demands coupled with living on a tight budget...ministry is not an easy choice, therefore in order to stick with it, it must be a calling from God alone. In describing our lives, there was so much positive, we have two wonderful Christian children, and their families both in ministry today. I recall my own learning problems as a child when I became a father. When my daughter and son were babies, I held them and read books to them, until they went to kindergarten. Today my son has his doctorate and is a pastor in a large Presbyterian Church in Wheaton, Illinois. My daughter has her master's degree with honors and is a children's minister in a large church in West Palm Beach, Florida and also teaches freshman English as a professor in a Christian University. My precious children have never known my fears. We had amazing times in ministry working in major churches with thousands of people. Our lives transformed through the joy of counseling other people, and building churches, pointing as many as we could to Jesus Christ. We both gave all we had to ministry with little time to relax, restore, refresh, or renew. We made the mistake of not giving attention to small things but only focused on the big things. Large programs, beautiful homes and neighborhoods, schools for our kids... but did not focus on each other like we should have. Because of this, we began a journey that led to great pain and sorrow and hence we could not fulfill each other's emotional, spiritual, and physical needs. Of course I must take the responsibility for a failed marriage because I can only judge myself. I will speak about what I learned from my divorce just a little later.

Going from a conservative Christian University to the tenderloin of San Francisco was like shock and more shock. I lived in a studio apartment on Franklin street. It was the period of Haight / Asbury, the antiwar movement, and the Hippy free love attitude, all happening at the same time. My residence was in the red light area of San Francisco. I got a job to work for Croker Citizens Bank on the main street of San Francisco. As I walked back from my work at 2am, I had to pass by the people of the night, the homeless, criminals, beggars, and the prostitutes. Where I came from, prostitutes did not exist. The gay bars and transvestites were also prevalent in those environs. I worked in the evenings from 6pm to 2, then had seminary class from 8am till noon...leaving me exhausted and feeling as if I was in a dark place with seemingly no way out. The walk to class on Van

Ness Ave started from 7:30am to make it there by 8. 1 was ready for a change.

Part of my seminary training was playing the trombone. One afternoon I was asked to play for the opening ceremonies of the seminaries new semester. I played without music (by ear), which I had done many times in the past. But this time, I slipped on a couple of notes. This was so embarrassing especially afterwards, when my (my new wife), Pat, questioned if I was called into the ministry . It definitely seemed after that experience that I would be marked as a loser. The next day, seminary classes passed quickly in spite of feeling like a loser, many people were still very kind to me...including the one student who asked me to play a trombone duet with him for the chapel.

On a Thursday morning, I received a call from a church in Brisbane, Ca. They asked me if I would be the special music person for their Valentine's Day banquet. I accepted, and my wife accompanied me on the piano. This event, changed my life drastically for the next several years. That very church, asked me to accept a paid position as their youth minister. Two weeks into my new job, the pastor of the Church took me and Pat out to lunch and asked if I would temporarily take over pastoring the church because he was leaving immediately. My life was moving too fast and I was unprepared for all of it. The mercy and grace of God allowed me to go with the flow for as long as I could.

Eventually, I was voted in to be the full time pastor of that church at the tender age of 23. Personally I felt very uneasy with this new responsibility and literally shook every Sunday, as I spoke . ...truly "All Shock Up," as the Elvis Presley's song goes. It was a church of 30 members with many nationalities which grew to 80. Their pot lucks were out of this world. It was a time when I became very comfortable ministering to all nationalities and races of people. To the point where I enjoy mostly ministering to red, yellow, black and white. I centered my attention on the young people that came from the projects....taking them to camp in the Santa Cruz Mountains, as their counselor. This got the attention of the Denomination and they asked me to be the recreational director for the high school state camp of 500 adolescents. Literally, all the activities had to be organized and cleared through me. During this amazing week, I had the privilege of meeting the music director from the largest church in the state. We made a brass trio with my trombone, his trumpet and Bob's (the staff member's) trumpet. It was an awesome week as such great connections took place. The next spring I was sitting in my office on a Saturday morning and the phone rang, it was the music minister of the Los Altos church. He asked me to be the Youth Pastor for the High School. We agreed, and that began one of the most exciting ministries I had ever had. Both the high school and college department memberships increased to 150 each, while some rallies numbered 500 in attendance.

Well, life seemed amazing from East Oakland to Los Altos. Having been thrust into state leadership, I had the largest ministry in the state for the denomination. I ran my own camp for the High School, which was a survival and water sky camp on Whiskey Town Lake.... spoke at several schools and colleges as special guest. Often I discipled kids to be leaders, and some became counselors for High School events. The combined group grew so large that we had the high school rallies in a gym, and the other in a college building we had built, in a similar structure. I thought my life was set forever, it was so wonderful. Even in my personal life, my little girl Rose entered kindergarten at the church and my son Joe stayed at home with his mom.

The senior pastors son who was the CE director for the church was threatened by the ever increasing size of my ministry, In addition to the fifty adult sponsors who worked with us. This man went to his father and persuaded him to split my ministry and hire another man with equal authority to take either the H.S. or college groups. I was so shocked, disappointed and hurt that I could not believe anyone would break something up, that was working so well. I learned not to take it personal, but prayed it would not be detrimental to the group of kids that were babes in Christ.

Through the transitions of my life I realized God is always at work, so that all things work together for good. He makes a way when I cannot see one. If God be for us who can be against us. Nothing can separate us from the love of God. I have tattooed these facts on my heart and when I see a dead end; God sees an opportunity to test our faith and pour us out a blessing that we cannot contain.

During this period of time, these amazing kids, grew close to the Lord, and changed their old way of thinking. Many of them found a true, real relationship with Jesus Christ and brought many friends to join the church. We witnessed our youth boldly living for Jesus and letting go of addictions and sexual immorality. It was a much needed move of God. After the CE Director split the groups up, I left after having served there seven years, sold my house and moved to a military town Seaside, California and started pastoring a little church of 35 people. In this small congregation, there had been dissention within the church involving the previous pastor, who had gone to Los Altos to be the seniors minister. In these transitions, I found myself relying on God's mercy, more than ever. I centered on the youth and music departments, in the church. And as a result, was able to build a youth group of 35 kids and three choirs which toured and sang in area churches. The church grew to 150 within the first year. No matter what church I was serving at, or what situation crossed my path, GOD intervened by opening up another each time one closed. He has never left me, and always turned the bad into good.

God also was giving me wisdom in my personal finances and investments. By His grace, I was able to sell my home in Sunnyvale, and then invest in two more homes... one in Monterey and one in Seaside. Then the opportunity came to sell those two houses, and buy two more. One was a beautiful home located near the Fisherman's Wharf in Monterey Hills. This place had a view of the wharf out of the family room windows, a view of the ocean out the living room, and Jack Peak State Park was our back yard. In addition, I also bought a small home in seaside with my youth minister as an investment. God gave me the ability and flexibly to seize financial opportunities of investment to help further the Kingdom of God and to provide for my family. I recall as a child being told by a teacher that I would only pass the class by the skin of my teeth, and in my innocence I went to a mirror to search for the skin on my teeth... now since I was jumping around (so much), from house to house, I examined my legs to see if they resembled a kangaroo's.

Religion always rears its ugly head trying to hinder the works of God. The deacons told me they wanted me to stop my work with youth and music. But, thank God, prior to this, I had been led by the Lord to write a letter to Clarence Sands, pastor of one of the largest churches in California. This church had a membership of 7 thousand, auditorium seated 3000, and had multiple services to accommodate. I simply told him in the letter, that if he needed me, to call me. Shortly after the deacons wanted to curtail my work with youth and music, my phone rang and it was Pastor Sands with a positive response. He said "this is Clarence Sands are you ready to join us?"

I went to his Church as the Executive Pastor and became the Interim Pastor after a year when the pastor retired. The church rallied and paid off some notes, and wanted me as the Pastor. Some, tried to bring in a big name pastor, but couldn't get a majority vote. So the pulpit committee asked me to make a public statement that I would decline to be the Pastorate of the church, so they could get their man. I agreed in order to keep the peace, and they did. It is no wonder Jesus says, He is coming back for a church without spot or wrinkle.... And from a pastors view, that unblemished church is a very small unselfish group... few and far between... awaiting HIS SUDDEN return.

Again, God intervened in a uncomfortable position and opened another door. A man came into my office one day and offered me the position to be the Pastor of a large Church in Los Gatos. I said yes, and accepted the position within a month.

The church was 175 people when I first came, but grew to over 400 within two years. I had purchased a beautiful home located in Aliso Creek with a pool, had a little mg sports car, a Terry Trailer, and was enjoying watching the church grow. I had many Pastor friends who were very well known and everything was wonderful! I sat by my pool one Saturday morning drinking coffee and thinking, I had my ducks in a row, my future was as bright as all outdoors. THEN, The Voice of the precious Holy Spirit spoke to me and said, "If I take everything from you, will you still serve Me?" and I said in my heart of hearts, Yes.

I was taking the church through a verse by verse study of the book of Ephesians, and had come to chapter 6. In my study office, I recall reading... " And be not drunk with wine wherein is excess, but be filled with the Holy Spirit." Suddenly, the Holy Spirit's presence filled the office... in such a state of joy and wellbeing, I said out loud, "Lord, I want this more than anything in the world. I could sit here for eternity in total joy, and I know there is an inner circle and I want to be in it." It was a joy beyond description, I wish I could describe it but it surpasses description. This encounter was as if the Lord was filling me with grace, strength and power to handle what was coming next...

Chapter 7

THE VALLEY OF THE SHADOW

11 am

Mother's Day

Embarrassing Moments

Psalm 90: 1 A prayer of Moses the man of God. Lord, you have been our dwelling place throughout all generations. Things were so good on the surface, but underneath was pure disaster. As a pastor, I knew I had to set an example of what Jesus would want us to do. So my confession now is of repentance toward my exwife whom I verbally degraded for so many years. As a young man I had never been taught the romance, love and respect that a husband should show his wife, hence I winged it. All women, no matter their faults, need their spouse to treat them with respect and appreciation. No marriage is perfect, no matter WHO the people are. Money, position, or fame has NO affect after a short while...and the true character of a person surfaces. No two people were created perfectly in sync, therefore it is inevitable for disagreements to happen. Its not the disagreement that causes trouble, it's the manner and motive in which it is handled. When a couple has children, this becomes even more important. Even as pastors and leaders in the church, marital problems exist. My wife at that time, was very gifted and talented in many ways. She had a good heart and a generous spirit. But, neither one of us was perfect...nor showed each other proper consideration. When I look at my life, I now see the good and not so good. Life can be full of chapters and each one must come to an end. As we page through our lives, we can wish the pages were and are sweeter. I know at times in my life there has been a foul odor from wrong choices, which I paid heavy consequences for. But, thank the Lord for his mercy, which is new every day, to overrule and override my sin, mercy that walked with me through these crises of wrong decisions, actions, and words. The Bible says, we get what we deserve and say, unless God intervenes through His grace, thusly, my life is an ongoing miracle of God's grace and mercy. There have been thousands of people in my life who have believed in me. I know it was not because I'm a phenomenal person but because of Gods favor on my life, to the extent that people overlook my faults and believe in my good. I guess the greatest illustration is when I was pastoring a mega church in Northern California. It was Mother's Day weekend. I spoke to my first wife at that time in such a cutting degrading way that she reacted by scratching my face. I then had to pay the price for my misbehavior. I thought my career and marriage WERE over that day, because I had to go to church and preach to thousands with scratches on my face. Make up never entered my mind back then, as a man, to cover the scratches... but rather I was ready to face whatever came my way. So, I went to church by myself, without my wife and children. As I arrived, friends and staff, greeted me in the church lobby all excited about that special day's events. One of them asked, "Pastor, what happened to your face?" And I answered, "My wife and I had a fight and she scratched my face." They all laughed and thought I was joking. I went on to my Sunday school class and as I stepped up in front of the large audience I announced, "I know you may all be looking at my face and wondering what happened... my wife and I had a fight and she scratched my face." They all burst out laughing, and the class went smooth. The next hour as I met all the staff in the greenroom for prayer, my secretary called me and said my wife was in the hospital with an anxiety attack. Our neighbor had taken her to emergency and was trying to get ahold of me. When my wife was handed the phone, I deeply apologized to her for having spoke to her in such a harsh way and told her everything was ok at church and with heartfelt contrition, I prayed with/ for her. Moments later, I did my best to minister to over 2000 people, also dedicated new babies with their families, and walked throughout the audience interviewing mothers giving them flowers... all of them staring at my scratched face. BUT, because I thought that everyone would find out my wife was in the hospital because of me yelling at her, I had a premonition that I would be fired soon... so I spoke as if it were my last service. There was complete liberty in that service. The pressure was off, and I ministered with a carefree spirit. God used that experience to usher in HIS anointing, and liberate His people. To this day, that very service is still spoke of as being one of the most anointed services of that church. What the devil intended for bad, GOD turned it for good! It was a memorable service... because, let's face it, I was a "broken man." God can intervene even when we are at our worst, and show Himself to be great, despite our weaknesses!

Two and one half years later, while pastoring in a different church, and during communion service, the Holy Spirit spoke to me that my wife was making plans to leave me. I went home that afternoon and asked her about it... and she said it was true. We decided to reconcile. I was very much in love with my wife, and felt desperate to keep her... desiring for no one else to have her. And one day in my frustration, I realized I had two feelings going on inside of me...one of deep love and the other of unforgiveness. I said to her, "I wish I knew earlier that you were planning to leave me, because I would have made plans of my own."

Obviously, I was my own worst enemy. In a moment of heat this statement came out. It showed me that unforgiveness was still buried under neath. My wife sensed that I was truly struggling to forgive her and still held resentment which drove her further away from me with no possibility of reconciliation. She then took up counseling to deal with our marital issues, and as a result, a friendship began with my wife and the counselor. This was the beginning of the darkest season of my life, and I thank God now for seeing me through it. Looking back, I recognize His Divine Intervention, numerous times. My wife at that time told me that I was to leave the house. I continued to pastor the church alone, staying briefly in the guest house of a close friend from the church. After resigning from the church, I went to the only place I knew to go without intruding on my friends... and that was a halfway house full of excons. Though I only stayed there less than a week, I so enjoyed their company as we read the Bible faithfully every night and prayed together for all of our circumstances... staying in agreement that God would make a way for us. As normal behavior during the drama of divorce, food is never attractive, so I ate sparingly and the guys were trying to get me to eat. I had only brought with me a car load of essentials and felt so helpless. Many a time, I begged God to take my life and welcome me home. My heart was broken and my career seemed to be over. The greatest pain I suffered was thinking about my two precious children. I remember driving my MG, with the top down trying to seek some form of peace, and ended up pulling the car over to the side of the road, weeping, and crying out to God, asking Him, what was going to happen to our precious children, whom at that time were 9 and 13. Immediately, The Lord spoke to me saying, "I brought Rose and Joe into the world, they are Mine, and you will have to trust Me to raise them." That was all I needed to hear.

Through this deep valley of mine, there was one lady who stuck by me, my cousin Linda who was my second sister. She not only walked me through that deep dark valley, but she was also the faithful one (years prior), who had helped me with my homework nearly every weekend through my high school years. There were people who acted as angels in my life during this time, and I thank God for their encouragement. God sent my precious cousin to comfort me when I needed it most. For the sake of other precious people out there who have been a victim of divorce and been ostracized by others in the process...this is for your benefit... I remember the nursery rhyme as a child: Humpty Dumpty sat on a wall, Humpty Dumpty had a great fall, all the kings horses and all the kings men could not put Humpty Dumpty together again. This describes the shock of divorce.... Realizing so clearly that something new must happen in your life because there is no turning back. Relationships are broken that will never be restored again (to be what they once were). I recall the day, my wife said she was going to divorce me. Immediately, I called a deacon's meeting that would follow the morning service. During the meeting, I bust into tears and shared what I was going through. I wept copiously until they heard all that I had been experiencing. In my broken spirit I assumed they were true brothers that would show sympathy and prayer. Instead each one of them got up and left without a word. I realized that these precious dear men whom had been my closest friends in ministry were no longer my friends, nor wanted anything to do with me again. Divorce brings a sifting into our lives. (Jesus told Peter that Satan wanted to sift him like sand., but that HE was praying for Peter, that he would come forth as gold.)" My life was being sifted. I held on to promises from God, "I will never leave you nor forsake you... I will stay closer than a brother." The following Saturday was a work day (at the church), and I came to encourage all those who were there and thank them for their support. But, the chairman of my board who was my closet friend in the church took me aside and said, "Pastor I don't know about the rest of the church , but I want you to resign now." I replied by saying that it would happen after the papers were filed out. Following that day, fear overwhelmed me both day and night. Each morning I would wake up and look at the ceiling and realized I was still alive and could not escape life's circumstances. I envisioned myself in the dark on a railroad track in a tunnel, seeing the light of a freight train coming straight at me. As I shook at my wedding, so I shook again in total dejection and despair. I was about to lose my joy, home, family, career and reputation. Many times I continued to beg God to welcome me home... thoughts of suicide crossed my mind as I desired to jump into the freeway... or smash my car, losing all hope to live. I moved into a trailer we owned for a time. At times, my daughter stayed with me and my son with his mother and her new husband. We had a cat and a dog as family pets. Just as I had experienced childhood grief with loosing Corky, so my son witnessed the loss of one pet and the demise of the other (which ran away). When he called me crying inconsolably, I understood completely what his grief felt like and sobbed with him. This valley in my life seemed to have no end, and was only getting worse as time went.

I tried to get a job but had no computer skills to land one in Silicon Valley. So the kids lived with their mother and I stayed with a couple I met in a covenant group at the church. They knew my situation and asked me to housesit. My ex and I still had two rentals in Pacific grove which had a little equity in them. I asked my EX and her new husband to please buy or sell them from me or to me, because I could not afford their payments, and did not want to wreck my credit. But I received no response. So, I had to sell my trailer and car in order to pay for an apartment to move into. My two rentals were headed into foreclosure.

But by the grace of God I was able to prepare them for selling, and they both sold just in time to spare my credit. By God's grace a friend gave me a cleaning job in which I took my kids on occasion, otherwise my exwife kept them. This little job and the sale of my Trailer, afforded me the funds to be able to rent a small studio apt in a nice area in Sunnyvale.

In addition to all of these transitions, I tried getting my life back together by attempting dating. It was not a pleasant experience to begin with, but I thought this one young lady could help bridge that void I needed filled so desperately. She was the type to sit on the front row of church and had a home in Los Altos. The chemistry was excellent and we discussed getting married. She had mentioned that we needed to fix up her home first (which was very run down), and then we could live there after marriage. So this, was my life for a while until one night when I came back from work to her home and discovered she was not there. I knew in my spirit that she was out on a date with someone else and I needed to get the strength to walk away. Sequestering myself in her shrubbery, I waited for her to come home. Late that night she pulled into the driveway with another man, stayed in the car for a bit, then kissed him, and invited him in for a time. Quietly, I remained hidden. There was no way, I needed to relive that nightmare again. So, I stayed until he left in order to maintain the proper time line for factual proof of her infidelity. It was heart breaking after spending so much money, time and effort, fixing up her house, only to be betrayed in such a nefarious way. I needed to witness that in order to convince myself she was not the one for me. The next day after church, I severed all ties with her, in spite of the fact that she was a sweet girl and very pretty.

Divorce can be expensive and nerve wracking. Many friends, family or associates would rather back off then take sides. The Bible says, rejoice when we are persecuted for His sake and that is what I felt was happening. Stories can sometimes travel and lead to gossip and untruths, as happens in many divorces, unfortunately. In any dramatic situation, little things can be exaggerated to disproportionate sizes, and I wondered back then if there would ever be light at the end of the tunnel. I had a part time job cleaning offices at night and one evening as I was cleaning bathrooms, I knelt beside the toilet and stared at the sponge in my hand, in deep thought of how my life had changed so drastically in such a short period of time. We all fall short in certain seasons of our lives and I remember an illustration I used once in a sermon. At times we may feel like the little girl who went to Sunday School for the first time and rode the church bus. In Sunday School they gave everyone their memory verse for the week on a small slip of paper, and this little darling had hers memorized before she got back on the bus to go home. Sitting by an open window, she held her paper which read, "have faith in God". Suddenly the wind blew and it was sucked out of her hand, and out the window. She jumped up in the center isle and shouted at the top of her voice, "Stop the bus, I've lost my faith in God." Dear precious people we all have times a tidal wave comes along in our lives and we go under and think we have lost our faith in God and for sure He has lost His Faith in us. But that's not what His Word says in John 10:2729. Jesus said here "my sheep listen to my voice, I know them, and they follow me. I give them eternal life, and they shall never perish, no one will snatch them out of my hand. My Father, who has given them to me, is greater than I, no one can snatch them out of my Father's hand." Any church or person who adds works and performance to Jesus' words is not speaking the truth and is a deceiver. My dear friends we must get secure in the Words of Jesus, that nothing can separate us from the Love of the Father when we have put our faith in Jesus. The Holy Spirit came and spoke this as loud as can be to hold me solid for all that was ahead in my life. HE knew the road would get rougher, but HE would carry me through. Though I have been caught at different times in the storms of life, and tossed about, my anchor still holds. I have never been shipwrecked by a storm and my course is set as I head for glory beyond human comprehension.

Sometime later, I went to a large church in which the pastor and I knew each other well. This was just to visit and get refreshed. I was sitting in the front row and enjoying the worship, when the pastor (my friend), walked right in front of me and would not acknowledge my presence. That same shunning carried on the entire service. So, I forced myself to focus on the worship, and this is an example I remember because although friends may turn on you, JESUS never does. The song lyrics says... DOES JESUS CARE? YES, HE DOES! As I realized that day, more than ever, HE is truly our closest friend. HE is there right in our midst, when we seem rejected and alone. Jesus truly cares, and will bring us through! I sobbed uncontrollably throughout the entire service, as the Lord was healing my heart. At the service's end, I left refreshed and focused on HIM, not others or my problems. I truly understand and forgave any and all people that innocently misunderstand stories that are/were told to them in the midst of a mess. It is not their fault, as most would rather stay out of the situations to avoid taking sides, or being caught in the middle... BUT JESUS purposely puts HIMSELF IN the MIDDLE of our messes...and turns them into MIRACLES! ALL things work together for good to those that love the Lord, and who are CALLED, according to HIS purpose.

Out of marriage and divorce, I must explain what I learned from these experiences, as a man and how to be a good husband. The foundation for marriage, is having a personal prayer (place) Altar! The best analogy I can use would be the example of a bank. If we look at our marriage as a bank and our spouse as an ATM. A wife MUST have regular deposits put into her spirit and soul, made with a minimum amount of withdrawals from us men. Every wife marries her husband because she believes in him, and believes that he will protect her, respect and be kind to her and her family. A wife will do everything in her ability to support her husband's visions, therefore the husband must constantly encourage her, thank her and show her she is the most important thing in his life. He must make deposits of kind loving words, gifts, and listening to her opinion... valuing what she says. If they have a disagreement, and it upsets her, he only has two choices...leave the house immediately to take a break, and not speak a negative word... or go to her and say, "I'm sorry, please forgive me, and tell me what needs to be done to resolve this. " It's that simple. Then follow the amendment up with regular gifts. These gifts, whether they be as small as flowers or as big as a house, will speak for us men, when we don't have the proper words to say what needs to be said. They say...I respect you, I believe in you, and I value you.

Chapter 8

ONE ON ONE WITH THE MASTER

3am

On My face

GOD SPOKE

Psalm 103: 13 Praise the LORD, my soul; all my inmost being, praise his holy name. Praise the LORD, my soul, and forget not all his benefits who forgives all your sins and heals all your diseases.

I was in my studio apartment arguing with God that my life was over, because of all the evil things people had done to sabotage my efforts . God did not reply to me audibly, but much louder than that... HE spoke to my very being my heart, soul and spirit and said "Jerry if you will forgive every one in the past, present, and future... and judge yourself only, as long as you live, I will make a way for you." I just fell to the floor and said, "Lord I love you, I trust my future to you and know you are going to take me to heaven someday. But I don't think you love me anymore and I can not go on unless I know you love me. I need you to show me you love me so I can get up and walk out the door and hold my head up high. Please show me you love me and give me a real job within 24 hours. Amazingly, my phone rang 12 hours later and it was a total stranger offering me a job, salary, benefits, a car, expenses, and commissions, and I said with extreme relief, "When can I start?" I knew God loved me from that day on because His presence and involvement in my life would deepen as I realized Jesus is the same yesterday today and forever...what He did for others, HE does for me too! God wants us to anticipate, and participate, which results in acceleration and intensification of HIS miracles... All proving the Love of God, which is beyond our comprehension. As Paul wrote "If God gave us His only Son how will He not also along with Him also give us everything." (Romans 8:32). Divine Intervention had taken place. The one thing that held my life together through my transitions of crisis was listening to worship music, but realized throughout the process that I needed to become a worshiper. So, I discovered a little Church that was meeting in an old super market. The people stood and raised their hands in worship which I loved. Though I didn't participate at that time, I enjoyed being among them.

The job entailed me selling glass to major companies. It was a huge success and I was able to save a lot of money. Tom hired me and became a dear friend who looked after me. We worked side by side and he trained me personally. The owner, president and management were so upset with him for hiring me that they forced him to resign and then plotted my dismissal as well. At first they kept me on the inside sales desk job, where I keep inventory. To stay calm throughout the day, I would go into the rest room and put my head in the sink's cool water. After months they were convinced I was the best they had ever hired, hence put me out into sales for the bay area and southern California. The president brought me in and said that he wanted a friend of his to have my position and that they had a major problem in completing a forty seven story high rise in down town San Francisco. He wanted me to go the Gavin company in Oakland every day to complete this job. God gave me favor with those people, and the wisdom to solved the problem of bent laminated glass. One of the things I had to do was go to see the manufactures of the bent laminated glass in order to understand how it was done. I drove through Mission Viejo, Ca to get there, and as I passed beautiful Mission Viejo Lake I had a vision of meeting a beautiful blonde that lived on the Lake. That trip paid off because I realized from my research how to solve the problem with the glass. The president of Gavin said he would give me the checks to take to the owner of our company to give me the credit for it...therefore, delivering 5 checks for a hundred thousand each. God blessed me in Havalin Witkin Glass Company and I was there for 7 years. Divine favor had been given to me as I made more money than I knew what to do with.

After three months with them, I was able to buy a home in San Jose that was in foreclose. Immediately I gathered my two children and gave them a new home to live in, and arranged through the help of friends to keep my son in his old school. Both children were doing well in their new environment and I was out of the valley of the shadows and nearing the mountain top.

On one of my trips to Southern Ca, I met with Tom and his wife Dee who had moved to Southern California. I asked them to pray for me that I needed a wife and my kids needed a mom. Dee said she knew of a young lady named Carol that was also single with two children. They asked if I would be willing to go on a blind date to meet her. Feeling so foolish, I agreed and the arrangements were made. When I saw Carol I thought she wouldn't want anything to do with me, so I didn't talk much, in order to guard my heart from rejection. After dinner Tom said he was taking us to the Disneyland Hotel where we could relax and dance if we wanted. I just went along for the ride, not knowing what would happen next. They purposely put Carol and I in the backseat to further the potential of a second date, and it worked. I sat quiet because of the invisible wall I had built around me until I realized she was actually interested in me. I could not believe it! As we became comfortable at the hotel I told Carol I had been raised Baptist and didn't know how to dance. But we tried anyway, and soon she asked me if we could stop dancing and sit down. It was during this talk that I realized she loved the Lord and that I needed to ask her on a second date. She agreed to go to Newport Beach with me for a whole day. It was a beautiful January Southern California day, and we went to Balboa Island and then on to Laguna Beach. She asked me to meet her sister and her husband and then take her home to her house on Mission Viejo Lake. I was all shook up because this was the vision coming to pass which I had months ago when driving past the lake. I asked her if it would be ok if I kissed her, and she said, "go ahead." The next Sunday we went to church together with Tom and Dee and it was a day to remember. On the way to take her home, I asked her to marry me, and she said YES! SIX WEEKS later, we were married up in Sacramento, California. I bought our house in Carmichael, which we still own. Her daughter Ann and my son Joe lived with us. Her son Ben stayed in southern California. He was 18 and had a very wellpaying job. My daughter Rose chose to stay in San Jose and live with her mom.

My new married life started as I worked for a branch of Havllin Witkin and taught in a large church which a friend of mine pastored. Carol my new wife was more deep into the things of God and wanted to attend a Pentecostal church which membered 10,000. I won that discussion because I was not comfortable with all that yet. At the same time, I was determined to respect my new wife in ways I had not in my previous marriage. Carol and I both worked and shared all the household duties together as well as the weekly shopping, and in doing so we realized working together, made things fun and there was no limit on what could be done. I did not want my new wife to deal with the stress of daily work, and I was pleased to carry her financially for the rest of our lives. One year later, we went to Carmel to celebrate our anniversary and it was there that I was introduced to worship music like I had never heard before, while watching pastor Jimmy Swaggart on TV. I had always turned him off but Carol left him on while I shaved in the bathroom. That day the Holy Spirit touched me through his worship music and I began to weep and walked out into the room holding my face in a towel, thinking I was having a nervous breakdown. That weekend we visited a church in Seaside that I had pastored, and then drove home enjoying one others company. It was a wonderful weekend. But it wasn't until a year later when we returned to that same hotel to celebrate our second anniversary and the exact same thing happened again. This time I came out of the bathroom with my face in the towel and sat on the bed as I heard the words penetrating my spirit; "In the last days I will pour my sprit out upon all men." I turned to Carol and said, "This amazing peace and inner healing, is assuredly the Holy Spirit of God, working in me... we need to go to a Pentecostal Church ...and we did!

My wife Carol and I then started a little church which grew to 75 members. We had a new home and two rental houses and a condo in Mission Viejo when we were asked to move to Mtn. View and accept a senior pastorate position there. This time, we prayed about it, and God said to do it, so we moved . My son Joe decided to move back with his mother upon our move to Mountain View. That separation was tough for all of us. Carol and I began pastoring the new little church which averaged 60 people. After two years it had grown to 90 and then to 200 with two services. God is a God of Increase!

Just recently, I attended a service where the pastor taught on the story of Joseph which is such an encouragement to see Gods intervention in Joseph's life, reminding us what He did for Joseph He will do for all of us if we believe... for He is the same yesterday today and forever. So it simply means there is nothing he has done in the past that he can't do today. It means we believe He will do it again. Joseph's life was nothing but success and rejection. God brings success and "religion" and condemnation brings rejection. Religion demands performance as a gage for judging our spirituality. We all fail at times which brings us full face with the mercy and grace of Jesus. This is God's plan to first humble us and then bless us. This is why communion in church or at home is so important. To remind ourselves that Jesus paid it all... and all to Him I owe. I am not to fear man or anything he can do to me, but to go from the negative to the positive and praise His name because surely something good is going to happen today. I believe perseverance as Joseph had, brings hope and hope never disappoints. It will take us to glory someday but for now it will make a way for us in any situation through God's divine intervention. Jesus said cast all your cares on me because I care about you. He said I will never leave you or forsake you. He will always show up at the right time. In the mean time we must praise His Name, we must worship in the good and bad times. It makes it a great adventure of signs wonders and miracles. God is in the business of miracles . He gets involved when we cry out from the depths of our souls "Lord have mercy." There is nothing like a miracle. If you have never had one surely you are going to get one soon.

I must also speak about a forgiving heart as I'm speaking about people that brought negative into my life. Through the power of the Word of God I am able to forgive them and judge myself in every situation.

I don't think about what they did, but think about what I did, in the circumstances. Never accomplish anything in the kingdom of God by responding to a negative with a negative, which I did too often in my life, but thank God things are different now. We can only please God by reacting to a negative with a positive, God have mercy on us all.

We may have to go through a series of transitions to produce a forgiving heart. Joseph had gone through all the transitions of his life before he came in contact with his brothers. In Genesis chapters 3750 we read how he was very cautious with them at first, testing their character to see who had changed and who had stayed the same. Then he was able to release his emotions with love and concern. He did say to them, "what you meant for evil, God turned for good."

If I could turn back the clock for a moment and share one of the most remarkable experiences I had ever lived to tell, it would be this amazing story. When I was a youth minister at the church in Los Altos, we had our own little house. My daughter Rose was 5 and my son Joe was 2 and life was wonderful. My father and mother drove across country, pulling their trailer from Florida to northern California where we were living. It was a wonderful time that Easter when my dad actually came to one of my services that Sunday morning. He and mom sat in the auditorium which seated 1200 people and saw me take part in the service. He then came to the afternoon musical and saw me play my trombone. After that, he walked down the aisle and hugged me. I was gushing inside as I had never seen this kind and concerned side of my father. He said to me, "I think I have died and gone to heaven." It was a wonderful visit as they stayed with us for two weeks. Wherever I went, he came with me, and took it all in like a sponge. He gave me the family silverware as a memoir. And as we were out in the back yard one day working on the door hinge, he began to cry and sat on the steps and put his head between his legs... weeping and spoke in total brokenness. "Please forgive me for not having the patience to teach you anything while you were growing up,." he said through his genuine tears. I was so shocked... nearly speechless for a moment then said, "Dad, I forgive you and I love you, and I'm ok." He left the next Sunday afternoon and before getting in the car, he kissed my children and wife first, then grabbed my face in his big hands and kissed me on the lips, looked me in the eyes and said, "If I was any prouder of you I would burst." He got in the car with mom and drove off. In just 5 weeks to follow that amazing visit, I was at the office and my phone rang... it was my sister. She said, "dad is in the hospital dying, his kidneys have stopped working, come quick." I got on a plane and flew to New York. My uncle Craig and aunt Gene picked me up and rushed me to the hospital. I walked into his room and the nurse told me he had just died. My mom was not there, she had MS and was at home in a wheel chair with my sister. I drove to my mother's home, where I cried deeply. He was only 56... it was overwhelming grief, due to just being reconciled with my dad and suddenly he was gone.

Mom asked me to speak at his funeral, because my dad had stated he wanted me to do so. It was the first funeral I had ever done. I was 29. I remembered my father's words to me throughout the years I lived at home saying, "Brub, I've got a sermon in my heart, I just can't get it out." I took his own words to give me the courage to give what would have been my father's sermon. He was a hell, raiser when he was young, then be came a new Christian when I was two, but he kept it all to himself. The church was packed out with the town windows, all his friends and relatives, and the church people. I shared some of the principles of his life, when he told me, "If God can forgive a wretched sinner like me, I can forgive anyone." I told the stories how my father insisted on order and holiness. First when he had caught an arsonist who was burning houses and barns down; by getting a print of his boot from the snow, went to his home with the sheriff to have him arrested. Second, when he had gone to the home of a former deacon in our church, who after his wife died molested three little girls... drove that deacon to the prison. Third, when he had gone to the home of one of our pastors who had gotten sexually involved with one of the high school girls and got his resignation, helping him leave the church. Fourth, when he went to the town pond when a little 6 year old boy had disappeared in the town, and with the volunteer fireman and the town people watching, walked into the ice covered pool in the shallow end, reached down through the ice until he found the little boy's body... picked it up and walked it to his parents. Yes, he was a person with short comings but he showed me through my life what it was to be a man. As I continue to turn back the clock, I recall when I decided to trap muskrat in the town creek one winter. I had never seen a muskrat so the first animal I found in my trap at 6am in the morning, I brought back to my parents' bedroom... woke them up and showed it to them. Dad said, "that's a rat." The next day I brought an animal into their bedroom he said, "that's a squirrel," the next day I brought the animal in and he said, "that's a mink... It's big money!" He was town clerk and wrote hunting licenses so he checked on mink season and saw I had caught it out of season. He took me to the game warden and made me give him my mink, and drove away. Then he said, "I should not have done that, he will just turn it in and get the money... but at least we did the right thing. All of these stories I shared at his funeral, then flew home to California to continue pastoring.

Returning now to the flow and order of God's Intervention throughout my life, the church I was pastoring was growing, and we were having two services, had a pastoral staff of four men, two of which were full time. I had combined a small church with ours and we sold their property for over 2 million so things were looking good for the future of the ministry. I was asked by the mayor of Mtn View to be on his development committee. The president of child evangelism was in my church and the head of the Gideon's Bible Society was also in the church. The SCSSC asked me to be a speaker and a local Christian television show asked me to do the morning devotional for the broadcast. So, I invited a guest speaker who shared that there was a second baptism of the Holy Spirit. Something I was not use to hearing, but craved to know more.

I was asked to meet with the chairman of my board of deacons and my music minister for breakfast. Prior to this I had been called by a Pastor friend who was pastoring a church in Portland Oregon. He had asked me to come as minister of Evangelism. I told him I had no peace about it, he said he would just wait, the job was mine whenever I wanted it. As I then sat at breakfast with these two men, my music minister said he needed to resign, he was part time, and I gave him my grace to go. The board chairman said he had called a meeting of the pastoral staff for Wednesday night to discuss a new direction for the church. I knew there was a stirring in my spirit to resign and accept the evangelistic position in Portland. So I shared with them at the meeting my plans, sold our home and moved to Portland as ministers of evangelism.

I loved that church dearly, and had a great vision of it being a major ministry in the bay area. My heart was broken. I decided to do something that I felt could change lives forever. We had many young people in the church I knew would have a great impact in the kingdom. So I wept through the first service sharing my heart and I wept through the second service as I told them we were leaving. I had people come up after the service and say they had never cried so hard in their lives as in that service. If my savior wept openly I felt I could do the same. I didn't want to do the religious thing , I wanted to do the natural thing. In the book of Isaiah, God says he will remove our hearts of stone and give us a heart of flesh. I had had a heart transplant on the floor in my studio when I received the message of God's love for me personally.

I went to Portland and my wife Carol stayed home to sell the house. It took three months. I had the wonderful privilege to live in a home with a couple named Helen and Henry during the three months. My son Joe came to Portland with the Azusa Choir for a concert and stayed with me at their home. My daughter Rose got married during that time and came to our home in the Bay area, to stay with us. My sister, her son, Carol's son and wife, Carol's daughter and granddaughter Kim. We all stayed together. It was a wonderful time and we still had our home in the Bay area to use for the occasion.

On Mothers Day Sunday, we still hadn't sold the house. So I decided to go to church and completely release all my heart in worship in the morning services to believe I could get God's attention and he would come and sell our house. David says in Ps. 103 Bless the Lord oh my soul and all that is within me bless His Holy Name. I released everything within me in worship that Mothers Day morning believing I could move the hand of God. Our house sold that afternoon. We bought a beautiful new home in Wilamette in the thick trees. While it was being completed Carol and I stayed with Helen and Henry. They became our spiritual parents from that time until they went to heaven. They were 70 and Henry lived to be 85 and Helen 99.

Often times, God will place people in your life that leave a permanent mark. A real friend who loves you through the mire and dirt. Real friends who love you better than a brother. Godsent people who are honored to help because their focus is to please God. And just the same, WE are placed in people's lives to bless them and help them on their way...knowing we will all end up in the same place very soon.

Chapter 9

OVERWHELMING FAVOR

6pm Sunday Service

Street People

Delivered and FREE

Psalm 107:1 Oh Give thanks to the LORD, for He is good; His mercy endures forever.

Throughout my life people have come along side me, believed in me, prayed for me and encouraged me. I always thought it was because I was an outstanding person who people liked. It's now at the short end of my life that I realized, it was the favor of God. God has sent people to see me from His perspective. It's been such a wonderful blessing and mercy from the Lord. Angels and Guardian Angels are watching over me. There is nothing in my personal being that would attract people....It's Christ in me the Hope of Glory that brings favor.

I have been in ministry 44 years... so busy for the Lord. Studying the Bible to preach it and found such joy in ministry and in the people.

While in Portland I became close friends with the Pastors father in law, who was a little Englishman about 5 ft. tall... a world healing evangelist...Mr. Price who was octogenarian at that time. He became critically ill and his daughter asked me to go visit and pray with him. He had an aneurism of the aorta and had bled internally for days and was extremely weak. That day he got dressed and I helped him into my car and we drove to a restaurant for tea and biscuits. The question he asked me as we ate was, "Jerry what is our purpose on this earth?" I said, "to glorify God," which was my standard answer. He replied, "no, our purpose is to Worship The Lord. You see, my purpose will never be hindered or changed by anything or anyone, because I can always worship the Lord." Then he opened his Bible and request I read Psalm chapter 24 out loud.

v.7... " lift up your heads, you gates; be lifted up, you ancient doors. That the King of glory may come in. Who is the King of glory? The Lord strong and mighty, the Lord mighty in battle." Worship brings the supernatural of God into our natural world.

The three ministries I had in Portland were awesome. Because of signs, wonders and miracles, the singles group were so numerous that they could not all fit in the room. I had made an agreement with anyone man or woman in our church, that we would believe together for them to find their spouse... that there was a man in her plan and or a wife for his life. And as a result of our prayers, I officiated twenty six marriages in the two and a half years I was there. Some wanted marriage but didn't have the money for a formal wedding so I married them in our Tuesday night meeting and gave them an offering as a wedding gift.

Each Sunday I would rise at 5:30am and relish in my study time and prayer, then open up the local coffee house going over my notes for that day. It was a surreal fleshly moment as I sat in that chair and patted myself on the back (in my mind), remembering all the wonderful things I had accomplished with this great personality and wit... when suddenly a still small voice spoke to me saying, "that was ME, with you, all through your life till this moment!' While starring at the steaming cup of coffee, my eyes swelled with tears as I wept uncontrollably. The presence of the Lord took over my emotions in that public place, to help me never forget that all good things come from God. You would guess that that presence would fade after a bit, but much to the contrary took place. As I drove to church, my eyes were still swelled with tears, and as I stood in front of the Sunday School class in the large gymnasium, again, I could not stop weeping. At the next service, the other pastors and staff laid hands on me thinking there was something wrong, as I continued to relish in the residue of His Holy presence. That morning and entire day, changed the way I thought about myself, forever. Yet the Holy spirit continued to remind me of this for years to come... as I recall sitting at another coffee shop one morning in orange county California, with an English healing evangelists! I again was speaking to him about my great abilities to minister and was wondering why God was not opening more doors for me. With a quiet reply, my English friend simply penned his thoughts on the back side of His tea bag and slid it under my nose. As I looked down to read what he wrote, the holy spirit took over my mind once again... It said, "God grant that I love THEE LORD, more than thy service". That precious man sat there with me with his hand on my shoulder for a very long time as my head rested in my hands, weeping bitterly. These supernatural encounters have occurred on numerous occasions in different states, cities and meetings... however I understand that many do not totally comprehend what I am writing about. The Bible says, the Holy Spirit is the one who reveals the workings of the supernatural world. God desires that we have a heart of flesh, and not of stone. (Ezekiel 36:26) What separates the heart of flesh from the heart of stone, is simply one thing... the filling of the Holy Spirit within any person's life. Some may use the excuse that they cannot be a part of the supernatural things of God because the Holy Spirit has not yet revealed it to them... but the truth is, when any of us read Gods word and ask the Holy Spirit to reveal His truth... because of humble yearning, the supernatural knowledge is given to us right then. The holy spirit is for all of us, just as Jesus Christ is for all of us... but God is seeking a hungry people that seek HIM FIRST!

People were healed delivered and saved through our meetings. There began to be manifestations in the ministry, one of them was people being slain in the spirit. I asked a dear friend, Mr. Boyd, a black pastor in the inter city of Portland to minister at our singles retreat. I will never forget , we began our morning service with worship... after the songs had been sung, he came up to the platform and asked, "how many people in this room are oppressed, or depressed: stand up and come forward." It was half the audience. He then put them all in a circle and began to stomp around them and shout, "I bind you satan in the name of Jesus, and command you out of these people's lives." Then after a short bit, he sent everyone back to their seats and began the service. He spoke on God's people being motivated, since we have been deputized through the blood of Jesus and handed our "spiritual gun, the Word of God," ...we are to use IT and speak IT into our lives and others.

Oft times, when ministers have deliverance service and command demons out, it is expected to have a counterattack because the gates of hell were shaken. But, that is why we have the blood of Jesus and the fire of the Holy Spirit to walk us through those attacks, so we can keep doing our job. Sometimes, however, we need backup in the natural as well, and God calls in another believer to pray with and for us. That is what happened to Mr. Boyd that Sunday. In the morning service he wounded the enemy and by the evening service, they had tried to stop his work through a sickness attach. But God sent me as his back up to strengthen him to finish what he started. So, the evening service began with a hour of worship and I noticed Mr. Boyd laying over a chair in the back of the room. I introduced him to the evening crowd and he came up the isle dragging the chair, telling everyone that he was very ill and would have to sit and preach that night. But God had me lay hands on him and pray for his recovery... and he did! Instantly he was energized and stood to preach. Those demons that were bothering him, left the building and never came back, as the healing anointing on me, from GOD, gave that powerful servant of God the boost he needed. He spoke a powerful message on the move of God and His sovereignty. He took the hand of a very reserved girl in the front row and ran her around the room, which is something she would have not chosen to do by herself. He then stopped to speak into the microphone when we realized he was NOT out of breath, but the young girl was... with a red face and panting, extremely embarrassed. Then he said, "we sometimes want to attempt resisting the sovereign hand of God in our own personal life, but God will still have His way." He illustrated this by running her around the room a second time where she collapsed in her chair. At the end, he gave an invitation while praying with every head bowed and all were standing. Carol and I went up front beside him with eyes closed, and when we opened our eyes, we were shocked to see the entire audience had been slain in the spirit, laying on the floor... in total brokenness to God. It was one of the most powerful supernatural services we had ever encountered. Many were set free of oppression, and depression, while others were commissioned into ministry. There were moaning's and groaning's in the spirit, coupled with that beautiful sound of hundreds crying out to God in true repentance and worship. That young girl that he had ran around the room was then running herself, and she continued until the meeting was over, and without stopping she wept with her eyes and hands pointed to heaven. In the next singles meeting, many shared what the Lord had done in the previous meeting. That young girl who ran around the room, stood and told her testimony that she had been molested by her father, and had woke up each morning depressed, but that day the anointing in that room broke all yokes and she was set free to forgive and live again.

During this season at the church, I held a twenty four hour prayer meeting for a week, I noticed one woman came in the back and got on her knees praying every day. The last day I asked her what she was praying for and she said her husband who was on cocaine and living in the streets of Portland. They owned a restaurant and had two twine teenage daughters. As a result of her faithful hours of intercessory prayer, her husband became saved and delivered from drugs the next week. Following his transformation, he began driving his new Mercedes back and forth from down town Portland, bringing street people to church. I told him that we would employ the church bus to bring the people in instead.

These precious lost souls were getting saved, baptized, delivered from addictions, and given new direction. However; the head pastor became very irked because these street people seemed to be tacky in appearance and some smelled. He then told us to seat the street people in the corners, or in the back of the auditorium, where no one could see them. So we did as he requested...but that did not stop the move of God and these precious street people of all ethnic and cultural backgrounds, filled the corners and back. We had several bus loads filling up the church with unloved souls searching for someone who cared. Church members were so moved by the transformation of these people, seeing their hunger for God, that they offered money to help this influx of lives being changed. Many said they had never seen such a move of compassion in the church.

A great work of the Holy Spirit was taking place but the head pastor seemed to be threatened and felt he was losing control of the church. He brought me into his study and told me he had several grievances with me. Foremost, he said he didn't realize I had such people skills when he brought me on board. Another, he expressed his displeasure with me talking in the office with everyone and buying icecream cones when he was out of the office and remarking that while the cat's way the mice plays. It was obvious, that the dear pastor was perhaps threatened in some way. I was in shock, because he was such a gifted dear friend and I would never want to upset him.

I wept bitterly, and said "we will be leaving the church, but we will leave as your friend." And he said, "yea, we are buds." It was December and we put our house up for sale, and it sold within three days, as a full offer, and 15 day escrow.... Divine Intervention. We were back in our home in California on January 2nd and immediately started pastoring a church in Stockton the first Sunday of the month. At this new church we were given a raise and a free cell phone, which we had never had before and an expense account.

The most important part of my day is to begin by reading the Bible with my wife and praying. We always end by praying the Lord's prayer. "For deliver us from evil for thine is the kingdom and the power and the glory forever, Amen." I need daily deliverance in order for the fruit of the Holy Spirit to be in my life. Galatians chapter 6 speaks Love, Joy, peace, patience, kindness, goodness, faithfulness, gentleness and selfcontrol... against such there is no law For the Love of God to be in my life. I Cor. 13 love is patient, love is kind it does not envy, it does not boast, it is not proud. It does not dishonor others,, it is not selfseeking, it is not easily angered, it keeps no record of wrongs. Love does not delight in evil but rejoices with the truth. It always protects always trusts, always hopes, always perseveres. Love never fails.

The Holy Spirit convicts me of my sin and corrects me . He does it without judgment, but in love. I can totally receive and listen when He speaks. I understand, I have mentioned people in my life who have been a great challenge to deal with, but cannot judge them. I must only judge myself, in what my actions and attitude should be.

Maybe many of the negative things that happen to me, perhaps took place because of something negative that I had done in word or deed. God knows, and I must always go to the altar and ask HIM for mercy in my life. The vast majority of people who have troubled me are actually good people... many of them better than me. It was a defining moment one afternoon while on my face before God, asking Him to have me see my enemies through HIS eyes. When he gave me that view, it was easier to forgive and bless because I saw them through the eyes of LOVE... and hence try to see God's perspective in everything.

It was amazing to see Gods transformation through HIS Divine Intervention, before and after my divorce... while in the valleys and the mountain tops. Ministering in varies churches, coupled with my sales ability to financially provide in order to minister in a greater way... brought me to a deeper level of appreciation for the power of the Holy Spirit and God's grace. When I thought I was losing, I was actually gaining.

Chapter 10

24 HOUR TURN AROUND

10am

Altar

Expected Miracle

Psalm 115:1 Not to us, LORD, not to us but to your name be the glory, because of your love and faithfulness.

Three of our kids lived in Southern California and our first grandbaby Kim had just been born so we moved to be near them. I was an Interim pastor at this church and was also hired at a new sales job (a high tech glass factory), in southern California. So I flew each weekend to Northern California to preach and worked in southern all week. It was at this point God taught us the miracle of multiplying our money His way. God's wisdom taught me how to sell and buy homes to keep us solvent... from selling the home in Portland and several others in California, that eventually brought us to searching for a home in Orange County. I needed to have all rentals maintain their agreement, in order to stay above water financially. An incident I recall was when one tenant could not pay. So instead of kicking them out, I called and prayed with them to never miss another payment. God Intervened again and that dear tenant never missed another payment till the loan was paid up three years later!

We were in a rental until the right house became available for purchase. The four of us, our daughter Rose and her husband, went house hunting and I put in an offer on what I believed was our next home, contingent on the release of our rental agreement. Unfortunately another couple liked the home as well and placed an offer without a contingency, so we assumed we were out. But, while sitting by the community pool at our rental town house, our realtor stopped by and shouted over the fence that they wanted to sell us their home and take over our lease. I jumped up and shouted, "Thank you Jesus!" By God's grace, we bought our home and the value tripled in fifteen years.

Our first year in house I lost my job. We had a weekly sales mtg. in which the boss had me pray at ending. Then one day, he announced the company was closing and we would all have to seek a job. I panicked inside as calmly as I could. Knowing that the hand of God was on my life, I immediately started reminding myself of all the times HE had intervened and got me out of a myriad of trying events. Somehow, I knew God would never leave me hanging, especially at that juncture in my life. Calling my pastor I told him the situation, and he said, "what are you going to do now?" I said, "trust in the lord with all my heart and lean not to my own understanding in all my ways acknowledge Him and He will direct my life..... would you pray for me please?" We had just bought the house and a new car. We had no job or income, living off of credit cards. Eventually, I found several part time jobs of which one was with a glass company to get new accounts in San Diego (commission only). Another was with a printing company, and the third was with a church. Carol quickly got three jobs as well... all babysitting, but one was as a nanny for a preemie baby weighing 2 lbs. We were in a frame of mind to trust God and work our heads off, until we were able to get ahead. bl did all the cooking because Carol was maxed. We made just enough to pay the bills. Many times my car would not start, so I had to park it on hills and inclines in order to push start it by popping the clutch. I didn't have a cell phone yet, so I used the customers phones. I took my book of the business cards for my acct, put it in the front seat by me, opened and prayed over each account in the heavenly language of the Holy Spirit, all the while I was driving. As a result, in 6 months at the glass company, I became the #1 sales person and was asked to sit with the owner at the Christmas banquet. The sales manager would swear and curse at me because his two best friends were also salesmen. But because of my new liaison with the owner, all attitudes changed for the better toward me as they watched the owner show me overwhelming favor. In months to come, I was offered a full time job with a church in San Juan Capistrano, for $35.000. Even though it was not near enough to cover our needs, I took it because I loved being in ministry. The pastor told me to work on my only day off, to make up the difference. So in order to supplement the income gap, I began working part time with another glass company for a percentage of sales. It was a perfect arrangement because my first commission check was $250.00. I was so happy! Carol chose to keep her job with the preemie baby and I kept the part time glass job for ten years. The church went through a building program while I was there, but they gave me a closet as an office in the old parsonage. They put me in charge of evangelism, singles, seniors, altars, parking, ushers, greeters and visitation. The church grew and went to two services about the same size as the Portland Church when they grew to a thousand. I was not official in this denomination, but only allowed to be a lay man because I had been divorced. Unfortunately, I was never allowed to preach , but the singles meeting on Tuesday night (as in Portland), became as large as the church's regular Wednesday night services.

A growth had developed in my stomach, but I believed it would be healed or I would go to heaven because I was already 55 and my dad had died at 56... so I was getting ready to go home to heaven. At one of the church services, a woman noticed I was having trouble standing for any length of time, so she asked my wife what was wrong. As Carol told her, she let us know it was only a hernia. In relief, I ran to the doctor and asked for surgery. But the doctor said we had to examine the area first to clarify the problem. Thank God, it was exactly as the lady had said and the surgery solved the problem. I guess it was not my time to go home. The hernia had developed from pushing my car the year before.

The pastor wanted to see me for a 6 months review in his office. He said he didn't know I had such strong people skills. He asked me to quite standing around talking to people, stop eating ice cream in the office, and so on....basically seven grievances. I cried and said, "I'm leaving and I'm leaving as your friend." I went to the altar that next Sunday night and prayed, "Lord put me where I belong." Monday morning my phone rang and it was a friend who was one of my college advisors from the Los Altos church whom had become the head of development at CBN. God used him that morning to answer my prayer. He had become a director of development for CBN/ Pat Robertson of the 700 Club. He asked me to come to CBN to work and visit with major donors, and needed an answer immediately if I wanted the position. Of course I could not say yes fast enough! He said I was hired that minute, and would give me all the time I needed to quit the church I was currently at, but needed me to be at a partners conference in Virginia Beach in two weeks. Within 14 days of my desperate prayer at the altar, I was serving communion to thousands, standing next to Pat Robertson in Virginia Beach.

My position there was to call on the high donors of CBN in half of the USA. I called on a couple in Santa Barbara, we went to lunch, and as we were driving they told me she was losing her eye sight and were dropping her off at the doctors. I reached over and placed my hands on her eyes and prayed a total body healing over her.

It was this kind of work that I loved doing... anything to serve God and bless people. It was a privi lege to meet people from all over the USA, agreeing with them in prayer for a miracle. I invited many to come back to CBN in Virginia Beach for conferences. That very couple I had prayed for months prior in the car, had attended the next conference. It was such a blessing to see how God had not only healed her eye sight but also her heart murmur. At the closing meeting on Sunday there was a time for testimonies of miracles and this couple got up and shared with all including Pat and the VP how God had healed her completely. The next week, Pat gave me a bonus and a raise after being there just under 6 months.

Pat Robinson spoke in chapel on Monday, following that Conference on CBN existing through signs, wonderers and miracles . I had finally come into a place that blended perfectly with my beliefs exactly where I belonged. I just want to stop and say, every good gift we have experienced in our lives and all favor comes from God. We must continually worship Him because God dwells in the praises of His people, and in His presents is the fullness of Joy... and the Joy of the Lord is our strength. As I traveled across time zones and stayed out for 12 days at a time, I began to experience extreme pains in my stomach for hours at a time. The director of development had told me that I did not have an expense account for anything except for hotels, car and $32.00 dollars a day to eat. Many months later however, I found out that this director was not telling me the truth, and was later removed from that ministry. But until I knew the truth, I believed my expenses were what he said, hence to save money , I would eat fast food and use what I could save to take partners out to eat. This situation started my intestinal problems. It was so severe that I checked into emergency late one night. After examination they said I had acid reflex disease which was incurable at that time, so I took a prescription which gave me some relief. We had a prayer mtg. at our home once a month to pray for my health and others. Dottie a 700 club partner called me requesting for her eye sight due to a brain tumor. She asked to drive to our monthly prayer meeting but was an hour and a half away. Dottie drove that night and we all agreed in prayer for her total healing The next day she went to the doctor and was told the tumor was gone! Following that, she and her husband drove out each month to meet with us. We continued to pray for my acid reflex, and for a man whose wife was in a mental ward (who had three children). Within months, his wife was totally delivered from depression and joined our prayer meeting. In my personal struggles, I had an ongoing battle with kidney stones for 17 years...suffered the same pain (as a woman in labor), many nights. Each time I thought I would never see the light of day, but had full assurance that if it were my time to go, I was on my way to glory.

There was a song I loved to sing through the years of my life. It went like this : Satan had me bound, Jesus set me free, satan had me bound, Jesus set me free, singing glory hallelujah, Jesus set me free. We cannot set ourselves free. We go through times of addition, anger, lack of health, lack of money, lack of anything happening in our lives. We must allow Jesus to send the angels of heaven and the Holy Spirit to set us free, for whom the Spirit Of God, has set free is free indeed. Please listen to me, God is working on our behalf's all the time, none stop, there is warfare in the air. We must release our faith and speak the word of God. No weapon formed against us can prosper. (Isaiah 54:17) Greater is He that is in us than He that is in the World. (1 John 4:4) For we fight NOT against flesh and blood, but against principalities and power, wicked spirits in heavenly places. (Ephesians 6). We must stand with those who have fought the battle before us. Danlel said "though He slay me yet I will serve Him." Shaddrack, Meshack and Abendigo said, "be it known to you oh king, our God is able to deliver us, but if he does not deliver us, we will still serve Him." We have nothing to lose and everything to gain. Jim Elliott , a missionary to South America who was martyred for witnessing Jesus, said, "He, is no fool who gives up what he cannot keep, to gain what he cannot lose." We must give up, we must surrender, we must trust Him. We must cry to Him who is the God of mercy and grace to help us in our time of need, no one else can, no one else cares, no one else loves us like Jesus. He alone is able to deliver us...so hold an, help is on the way.

Do not give up... Just get out of bed, take a shower, get dressed and report for duty. I visited a couple in Tucson, Az who had a copper warehouse business, prayed with them, the Holy Spirit touched them, and they gave generously to God's kingdom. Their business grew to where they were multimillionaires. Then I visited a couple who lived in Silicon Valley, went to their home and prayed with them. He had a hi tech business , which exploded after they gave over a million to the work of God. CBN promoted me to a higher level and I was most definitely in the perfect will of God for my life. Carol and I were in Fashion Island, Ca for the High Donors meeting when the presence of the Lord filled the atmosphere, and this standing room only gathering turned from a testimonial into an anointed healing service. It was an unforgettable event. However, that night, I realized I had lost my wallet. Carol and I had searched the room from top to bottom, and found nothing. Retracing my steps from A to Z, I went to bed unsettled because I could not locate it, nor was able to cancel my credit cards at that time. The only thing left to do was pray. Peace came over me and I went to sleep. After a good night's rest I got up early, went out of the room and made calls to cancel my credit cards. I came back in the room and opened the curtains. Just then a beam of sun light came in and lit up the carpet and there on the floor in the center of the room was my wallet. Divine intervention an absolute miracle!

Chapter 11

INTERMISSION

5:30 am

Alone with the Holy Spirit

Forgiveness and Repentance Come Easy

Psalm 121:12

I lift up my eyes to the mountains where does my help come from? My help comes from the LORD, the Maker of heaven and earth.

Having shared of such a great miracles throughout my life, let's talk about vails. Moses came down from the mountain and his face shown so brightly that they couldn't look at him, so they put a vail over his face like a mask in order to look at him. Later the glory of God, shining on his face went away and he still wore the vall, making everyone think he still had the glory of the Lord. We are all sinners saved by grace with the new nature, still having to control the old sinful nature. There is no hope in our mistakes but an altar of brokenness to receive grace and mercy from God, in the time of need.

For years I loved cowboy movies... the good guys wore white hats the bad guys wore black hats. I have a white hat and a black hat. As I have been writing my life's experiences as a public figure, vulnerable to unexpected trials, I do not want you to think I'm the good guy and all these people were the bad guys. Actually, my exwife and all the ministers were good people. They supported me, yet, I'm sure they had good reasons to take issue with me. It is imperative that I do not make myself look infallible, because I am nothing but a sinner saved by grace. All the Christians I have mentioned in this book are better people than me. I was privilege to know them.

I desired to write a kingdom book that lifts up a perfect Savior. All the interventions in my life were brought about by the mercy and grace of God... they were not in any way what I deserved. Carol and I have been married for 30+ years not because I'm a good husband, but rather because she is such an amazing wife. Carol is a person of peace, love and grace.

I would hope this true life story would show encouragement through the mountains of success and the valleys of failure...knowing that Jesus is the same yesterday , today and forever. And what he did to help us through the last trial, he will do again. He is our only hope. He is the author and the finisher of our faith. Just as He intervened in Esther's life by giving her favor, wisdom and arranging circumstances to eliminate her enemy and spare her people, so God is making a way for each of us to conquer our circumstances. We must submit to God in whatever way He tells us; for Esther it was that she should fast and pray. He speaks to each of us personally and deals with us personally because He is a personal Savior. We must trust Him.

TRUSTING GOD comes after you get to know Him. We learn about Him, from reading the Bible and praying every day. It's a game changer. It will allow us to hit a home run. Bake the perfect pie. Have the will power to do the right thing in every circumstance, and run from evil.

Chapter 12

THE SUPERNATURAL IN MINISTRY AND MONEY BURGEONED

7am

Sudden Change

Destiny Settled

Psalm 139:1316

For you created my inmost being, you knit me together in my mother's womb.

I praise you because I am fearfully and wonderfully made; your works are wonderful,

I know that full well. My frame was not hidden from you when I was made in the secret place, when I was woven together in the depths of the earth. Your eyes saw my unformed body; all the days ordained for me were written in your book before one of them came to be. How precious to me are your thoughts, God! How vast is the sum of them!

I worked for CBN for a very long good time. Having great results, they continued to give me raises and bonuses. I have never worked with a ministry that was so kind and generous, giving and gracious, in all my life. Yes, other ministries offered me to work for them as well, some I accepted and others I did not. But through all this, I realized I had reached a point of destiny. Pat Robertson is perhaps the humblest man I have ever known next to Billy Graham.

The Lord had given me great wisdom in how to multiply money and live debt free. Houses, cars, and accessories were able to be paid off, and bank notes increased in value. My wife had so patiently weathered through such a whirlwind of church jobs, that I chose to bless her in more ways than one, and one of those was buying her a beautiful Mercedes. There is nothing I would not do for her. On another occasion, the Lord showed me to take a line of credit from the house and place it in a bank note... within three months it multiplied 7 times itself. I sold it, paid off the credit line, bought things and invested more. However, I have, by God's grace become very prosperous, I am more grateful for prosperity of soul and spirit... than any material gain. All of this is NOT mine, for He has just given it to me temporarily. Therefore, whatever we give back to God, we are only returning to HIM, what He has already given for us. The earth is the Lords and the fullness thereof.

These two following wisdom keys from our Earthly Instructions Book (Bible), have given us examples of multiplying what God has given us but also being willing to walk away from it... knowing that the GIVER is greater than the gift. This mature realization helps us balance the beauty of success and obtain wealth without the wealth obtaining us.

Philippians 3:8 Yea doubtless, and I count all things but loss for the excellency of the knowledge of Christ Jesus my Lord: for whom I have suffered the loss of all things, and do count them but dung, that I may win Christ...

The Parable of the Talents

Matthew 24:1330

This story applies to all of us, in a natural way and a supernatural way.

14 "For it will be like a man going on a journey, who called his servants and entrusted to them his property. 15 To one he gave five talents, to another two, to another one, to each according to his ability. Then he went away. 16 He who had received the five talents went at once and traded with them, and he made five talents more. 17 So also he who had the two

talents made two talents more. 18 But he who had received the one talent went and dug in the ground and hid his master's money. 19 Now after a long time the master of those servants came and settled accounts with them. 20 And he who had received the five talents came forward, bringing five talents more, saying, 'Master, you delivered to me five talents; here I have made five talents more.' 21 His master said to him, 'Well done, good and faithful servant. (c) You have been faithful over a little; I will set you over much. Enter into the joy of your master.' 22 And he also who had the two talents came forward, saying, 'Master, you delivered to me two talents; here I have made two talents more.' 23 His master said to him, 'Well done, good and faithful servant. You have been faithful over a little; I will set you over much. Enter into the joy of your master. 24 He also who had received the one talent came forward, saying, 'Master, I knew you to be a hard man, reaping where you did not sow, and gathering where you scattered no seed, 25 so I was afraid, and I went and hid your talent in the ground. Here you have what is yours." 26 But his master answered him, You wicked and slothful servant! You knew that I reap where I have not sown and gather where I scattered no seed? 27 Then you ought to have invested my money with the bankers, and at my coming I should have received what was my own with interest. 28 So take the talent from him and give it to him who has the ten talents. 29 For to everyone who has will more be given, and he will have an abundance. But from the one who has not, even what he has will be taken away. 30 And cast the worth less servant into the outer darkness. In that place there will be weeping and gnashing of teeth.'

To glaze over our lives from an eagles point of view we can take a look at so many powerful people of the Bible that lived it before us. God knew their testimony was so valuable for each of us to learn from or live by today. Each of these people reached their destiny and lived long enough to relish in it.

Joseph was one of them, Job was another, Esther, Hannah, Mary, Daniel, Shadrach, Meshach, Abednego, and Paul to name a few. We as pastors tend to preach on the trials of those in the Bible, BUT, the last half of their lives is what I choose to focus on today. This message is for all of us who have been through enough and are ready for a better beginning.

...... Once Joseph walked out of those prison doors for the last time... he never had to return! Living out the rest of his days with more power, money and peace than he had ever imagined. Not to mention, reuniting with his earthly father, relished a one on one audience with God Almighty, and had the privilege of allowing his once sworn enemies to see his overwhelming success yet humbly forgiving them and blessed them with grace and mercy. (Genesis chapters 41 50) His destiny settled!

.... Job, once his horrifying trial ended, he NEVER had to relive a bad day in his life. He not only got back what he lost, but God doubled it. Since he did it for Job, he does it for us! (Job chapter 42) His destiny settled!

.... Once Esther and Mordechai's nightmare was over, they never had to live in fear again, but rather were abundantly blessed beyond their comprehension till their time on earth had ended. (Esther chapters 810) Their destiny settled!

.... Hannah, once she made a promise to give up her first son to work with and for God, she was blessed beyond her imagination with more children than she had asked for. All of her dreams came true and she reached her destiny! (1 & II Samuel)

.... Daniel, once he came out of the lion's den, he never had to reenter again. He was given more power, favor and plenty for all of his days and his enemies were destroyed immediately. (Daniel chapter 6). His destiny settled!

.... Shadrach, Meshach, Abednego, once they stepped into the firey furnace, the SON OF GOD stood with them... and their lives were never the same again. They came out without a singe on them and were immediately promoted to power. Their trial caused hundreds of thousands to be ordered to accept the God of Abraham Isaac and Jacob as their only God, and ultimately saved the soul of a King. Their destiny settled! (Daniel chapter 3)

.... Once the Pharisee Saul had his heaven encounter, and became Paul, he never returned to being a murderer again. His past was over, and all the saints who had prayed for his true conversion received their answered prayer with extreme abundance as this con and excon wrote 3/4 of the New Testament for us to live by. Paul had reached his destiny and had more peace and contentment in serving the Most High God, than he ever had when he was wealthy and powerful. These books are to his credit in penning the voice of the Holy Spirit within him. His destiny settled!

Romans

1Corinthians 2Corinthians Galatians Ephesians Philippians Colossians 2Thessalonians

2Thessalonians 1Timothy 2Timothy Titus Philemon

Chapter 13

SECOND CHANCE

8pm

Church Camp

4 Amazing Youth

Psalm 103:3 He Forgives all our sins and heals all our diseases.

Everyone desires a second chance. Many don't get it and others won't give it. But I know that The King Of Glory gives second chances. As Billy Graham has said, "Keep on keeping on." The only way we can do that is through God, not people giving us second chances. We may not even believe we deserve a second chance, but God will give it to us anyway! (Jonah 3:1) Then the word of the Lord came to Jonah a second time. After being swallowed by a whale, and spit on the shore all bleached out, God gave him a second chance to do what he was instructed to do in the first place.

How many chances should someone get? Well, how many would you like personally? Jesus answered this emphatically with the woman at the well. Jn. 4:4 Why would Jesus choose to go through Samaria? Well, He wanted to give a "seventh chance" to a rejected dear woman who had a heart to know Him. Jesus on his way to Galilee walked to Sychar, Samaria and was so tired he sat down at Jacob's well. A woman came to the well, whom we know to be the Samaritan woman. Jesus spoke to her and asked for water and she says, I'm an Samaritan, you are a Jew... why are we talking. He wanted her to know that he was talking to the Messiah and that HIS water lasts forever. Jesus went into a rejected town and spoke with a rejected woman whom had not only been divorced five times, but was living in adultery, and chose her to be his witness throughout Samaria. This precious lady needed a seventh chance and got it! He saw her heart, and man saw her outward life. God sees our heart and man sees our outward appearance. Luke 16:15. As a result of Jesus' fasting and witnessing that day. many in Samaria came to know Him as Messiah! This precious divorced woman, needed the Holy Spirit and Jesus pointed that out to her clearly. The Blessed Holy Spirit of God would soon breathe new life into her, to give her joy unspeakable and full of glory, to fully understand with confidence that she was loved and given a 7th chancel Through the Holy Spirit the father seeks true worshippers. To do this we must be taken to the potter's wheel and be ground to dust. All our selfconfidence has to be ground to dust. Then the potter takes the dust in his hands with the wa ter of the word and makes a vessel of honor to worship and service. We are only made to contain the treasure of the Holy Spirit to light us up.

One of the hardest things I went through as an assistant youth minister at my summer High School and College camp, (which ran around 300 combined), involved a dramatic experience with four high school youth. At my summer camp I had invited my boss, the senior pastor of that church to be our guest speaker each year. Though it was my camp, I respected his opinion and he was the final say. The drama began when one student was caught smoking and easily reported three other girls who were supposedly smoking too. The head pastor and I discussed that we would give these kids a second chance if they brought all the cigarettes to us to destroy. Otherwise they would be sent home. These scared, humble kids not only repented but brought us all their cigarettes. I thought all was well at that point until the head pastor changed his mind and told me to wake up the kids early the next morning, place them on a greyhound bus to go home. I was devastated, because I knew how it would affect the kids. The kids panicked as they knew they had been betrayed and did not want to face any consequences. This was most definitely NOT my decision as I am very cautious to always forgive people and see their good, giving them chance after chance. I have been put to this test many times, and enjoy following the footsteps of Jesus, though I am far from perfect myself. Unfortunately this situation affected these four kids spiritually and mentally for years. And I eventually left that church the next year. Then just two years ago, the youth group held a reunion in which I was invited, and one of the girls who was sent home that awful day, told me later that she finally forgave me and was in total peace with the Lord. I watched her in our worship services at that reunion and her hands were in the air in total release. The Holy Spirit had come to give her a second chance and teach her to worship in Spirit and in Truth.

Chapter 14

DELIVERANCE IN HIS PRESENCE

7pm

Slain in The Spirit

For Hours

Psalm 16:11 You will show me the path of life; In Your presence is fullness of joy; At Your right hand are pleasures forevermore.

Toward the end of my time with CBN the director arranged for any in development to go to Catch The Fire in Toronto Canada... it was not required , just an invitation. I decided to go. This meeting was like nothing I had ever experience before or since, for me personally. It was a great deliverance meeting so there were a lot of manifestations happening, including laughing and falling on the floor. I had gone to the morning, and afternoon meetings and was then in an evening service. I was just worshipping and taking the time to refill my spirit man. That hot July night I shared it with a friend from CBN. The worship became so intense that I turned to my friend and said, "there is going to be a water fight in this room." Everyone had water bottles because of the heat. I had just spoken those words, and suddenly the people behind me emptied their water bottles on my head. I was soaked. Immediately, I began to laugh uncontrollably from my stomach, and could not stand to my feet. This continue for the rest of the evening throughout the service until all strength was gone. I laid in the seat with my head over the back of the chair and my mouth wide open with eyes closed. Then I heard the voice of a woman say, "you must have the fillings removed from all your teeth, because they are harmful." And then a second woman said, "God has done a great work in your life tonight... this is the beginning of your destiny!"

We went back to CBN and gave a report, and they made the decision to schedule a meeting of catch the fire at CBN. I went, and took some friends Judy and Rich , a very classy wealthy couple who wanted to see the power of God for themselves. Sitting in the front row, Judy grabbed the hand of the woman standing next to her and they both immediately fell straight down to the floor. The following day's service, I found myself so tired that I stayed seated... slain forward in the seat and howled (cried in sheer brokenness), just as I had done in the Pastor's meeting in Oregon

. I couldn't get up and couldn't stop crying. Rich bent over beside me and asked me if I needed anything, I remember saying, "Kleenex." It was one of the most humiliating in the natural, yet liberating in the spirit, experiences, I have ever had. God was speaking to me and saying He is going to do a great last day ministry outside the walls of denominations and He wanted me to be a part of it! This Word from the Lord came to pass as I was blessed to be apart of two of the largest international television ministries in the world, one of which was a huge healing ministry and CBN.

I was in palm beach for a family event looking at the lake and the holy spirit reminded me of a phone call I had received days prior. That man had offered me a job with IBS. Upon returning his call, I was hired within the month and enjoyed working in development with a ministry that was spreading Bibles throughout the world. This was one of the great privileges of my life. One of the men who helped support printing those Bibles, had an orchard in the San Diego Hills. His wife had just died so he was very broken. Carol and I went to see him every month and take him out to lunch. One time we were with him and he took us in an older pickup truck up one of the slanted steep hills to show us his big beautiful house that he had built for his wife. He said he was selling his truck because it was standard shift and he couldn't drive it that well, but nonetheless we were all in it driving up the hill to his house... when the motor stalled. It was a narrow dirt road at the steepest part of the climb and he got confused and started pushing the clutch down rather than the brake... we came within inches of going over the side of the road to sure disaster. By God's grace I put my foot on the brake and stopped the truck from falling over the edge. I pulled the emergency break next, put the truck in gear and pulled the clutch then asked for permission to get my wife and I out of the truck. There hung the truck, someone would have to pull it back on the road . Divine intervention through divine anointing to do the right thing at the right time, or we would have rolled down the hill... killing all three of us.

The presidential prayer breakfast took place and I was able to be a part of it, meeting with one of the most amazing presidents the USA has had, President George W. Bush. On another occasion, I was able to meet Billy Graham, which absolutely made my year! I enjoyed working with the Bible Ministry for two years when another major ministries called me back to help them, and again because I love the presence of God's power, I agreed. I was 64. It's amazing how I never grew tired of working for any of these ministries, despite difficulty or disappointment... but for the LOVE of serving GOD, I will serve him in any way I can until the day I take my last breath on earth. All ministry is a matter of faith, just trust the Lord, in whatever He asks you to do. God opened yet another door for me where a Philippino couple asked me to open a church in their office building complex. So we started, "Word of Life Bible Fellowship." We never missed a Sunday and the Lord's presence was always there in the meetings.

In addition I was asked to work with a Christian Radio Ministry, and I did, at the age of 67! This same radio ministry was the one my father listened to when I was a young boy. It was the second oldest radio ministry in the USA. Finally my body was speaking to me to give it some rest and this is what it said... I had been misdiagnosis with acid reflex when I had a gallbladder problem. I was passing gallstones for 16 years going through unbelievable lingering pain. My last Sunday to preach before going to the hospital, I recall telling Carol I thought I would die before the service was over. That night I went into an extreme attack and Carol drove me to emergency. I was put on I V and monitored for the first twelve hours, then put through an MRI and an Ultra sound. The doctor came into my room and said you have extreme case of pancreatitis, your numbers are supposed to be 50 and they are 1000. My father had died of pancreatitis at 56 so I knew this was the end... I simply rolled over and said in my heart, "Lord thank you for a wonderful life, I am so excited to come home and be with you... but if there's still something I should do before I come, then heal me please so I can finish my work here on earth." The next morning the doctor came in and said your numbers are normal , we are going to get you on solid food and release you. Someone here will then schedule to have your gallbladder taken out soon. Immediately I asked my 8 children (4 kids and their spouses) and our 9 grandchildren to pray for me. We had agreement for healing and it was done.

Before the scheduled surgery date, one of my daughter's had asked me to come to her graduation... she was getting her master's degree at 39 years old. So I left immediately for West Palm Beach. But while there, my wife and I had a call from the doctor's office saying, I needed to get my surgery immediately because they found a spot on my liver. Without fear, my wife and I prayed that I would make it to the other side of this trial with complete healing. Within five days I was in surgery. The day after, the doctor called and asked how I was doing...I told him I was feeling great. He was amazed, because he said that was the worse gallbladder case he had ever worked on. He explained how certain areas of my insides were shredded from passing so many stones. Then, those precious words came that I will always remember, when he said, " I want you to know you have been given a new lease on life." But I still had to get the exam, for the spot on my liver. Days later as I sat in the hospital lobby waiting for my liver exam, when I heard a voice saying, " Jerry." Looking around I saw Bob, a board member of my church, who was at the hos pital for the last stages of cancer. He had gone through two years of treatment and was not afraid to die, but loved life nonetheless. We sat and talked for a few minutes... I went in for my test and was found to have a benign cyst, and he went in only to be transferred to emergency for the lasts days of his life. I remember going to see him, looking straight in his eyes, I realized his big blue eyes would be shortly be looking into the eyes of Jesus. As I officiated his funeral, I recall such a joyous spirit in that place. Both levels of rooms were packed and people were not sad and gloomy. They knew where he was and many yearned to get a taste of it! What a day of rejoicing we had in the presence of God. He is so wonderful . I am now 70 and am still reporting for duty.

Chapter 15

THE POWER OF AGREEMENT

Matthew 18:19 "Again, truly I tell you that if two of you on earth agree about anything they ask for, it will be done for them by my Father in heaven."

All we need in life is the presence of Jesus. He is the healer, the provider, the comforter, the protector, our righteousness.

What is important is to get someone to be in agreement with you. Jesus says two or three. Many times we are running in circles going nowhere because we do not understand the value of getting a person in agreement with you that the Word of God is the revelation of reality. If you are sick, claim a healing scripture together with someone if you don't have enough money claim a scripture on finance with someone. If you or someone you know (including yourself), needs deliverance, claim a scripture on deliverance with someone you trust. I heard Oral Roberts speak on a Monday night just weeks before he went to heaven. I was sitting in the front row only a few feet from Him because God wanted to bless me real big. His message that night was the scripture verse "no weapon formed against you can prosper" He made the emphasis that it is impossible for any weapon that satan has made to come against us can prosper. We are talking divine intervention. I did NOT know what spiritual warfare was, until I lost everything after living a blessed life of total success. I had preached Heaven and Hell, Angels and demons, but it was more of a theological position than a fact until I actually lived it out. What I lacked was a fighting spirit because I did not know who my enemies were. The world, the cosmos system of this world.... where Satan is the prince of the power of the air... sinful flesh, the old nature, mine and others. The Devil. John. 10:10 Jesus says, I have come to give you life and to give it to you more abundantly, but the thief, Satan comes to deceive, to steal and destroy. For we wrestle not against flesh and blood, but against "principalities, against powers, against "the rulers of the darkness of this world, against spiritual wickedness in high places." Eph.6:12 So we must be strong in the Lord, and in the power of his might. Putting on the WHOLE armor of God! Christians must agree on the Word of God and in particular what I have just quoted. There is unlimited power in the prayer of agreement.

Chapter 16

RUN TO THE ALTAR

Jer 33:3 Call unto Me and I will Show You Great and Mighty Things That You Do Not Know.

Whitney Houston sang the song in the movie "The Preacher Wife" "I Love The Lord" come on know you must get in agreement with me right now in what she sang. It was Ps.116:12 I love the Lord, for he heard my cry and pitied every wrong, Long as I live and troubles arise, I'll has ten to His Throne." If I ever heard an angel sing it, it was Whitney. There is a total release from her inward soul to the Lord. That's why we must have altars. There is no release without an altar. I never saw a "true altar," until I was 40 and went to an awesome church in Sacramento, then another one at an AG church in San Jose in which I had such a release, I could hardly walk back to my seat. That broken spirit of a dependent person on God alone is WHAT HE NEEDS in order to really use us.

God said in Psalm 51:17 "the sacrifices of God are a broken spirit and a broken and contrite heartThese Oh God You will not despise." The coral music of Moses Hogan entitled, Lord I want to be a Christian in my heart. Our hearts must be broken so we must turn immediately to God in times of crisis. In order to do this, there must be an altar in our heart where we can kneel and release all our burdens and cares in his hands.

Chapter 17

CONNECTING WITH THE SOVERGN KING

Isaiah 55:6 Seek The Lord While He May Be Found.... call on Him while HE is NEAR!

Some people have difficulty accepting the sovereignty of God. He is Omniscient, Omnipresent, and Omnipotent. He is all knowing, all present and all powerful. An altar is the place to go to acknowledge this. Jesus said in this world you will have tribulation but be of good cheer I have overcome the world. There is nothing God cannot handle. There is nothing God doesn't know... there is nowhere God is not present. Coming to a place of breaking inwardly to accept this fact, is the place of the anointing of the Holy Spirit... A place of going from the natural to the supernatural...A place that divine breakthrough begins in our lives.

CONCLUSION

There is joy unspeakable and full of glory and it's not through controlling our own lives, or living to please ourselves. I did not ask for these life transitions, but they just came one after another. Through them all He gave me was joy and fellowship with HIM. He's all we need. He's everything and He's free to all. Jesus' brother James said it this way, Come near to God and he will come near to you... Wash your hands, you sinners and purify your heats, you doubleminded. Grieve, mourn and wail. Change your laughter to mourning and your joy to gloom. Humble ourselves before the Lord , and he will lift you up. James 4:710

As we stay humble something good is going to happen to us. The Lord will lift us up. I didn't write this because I want to be somebody, I have everything in Jesus. I did not write this because I want to judge anyone but myself. Therefore, all the people who have come into my life, I desire them to be blessed of the Lord and make it to heaven!

There comes a time in a true believers life that their destiny settles. The trials and hurts are over as they thank God for HIS many Divine Interventions. The blessings overflow, and the abundance never stops. What HE did for Joseph, Job, Hannah, Esther, Mordecai, Daniel, Shadrach, Meshach, Abednego, Paul and many more, HE still does today... for I AM the same yesterday, today and forever! I pray this book ignites fire in your spirit to remember and appreciate every Divine Intervention God so graciously supplied in your life and confidently walk into your destiny and watch it settle. (Hebrews 13:8)

Let's just go to an altar and in agreement pray Jude 24.... To him who is able to keep you from falling and to present you before his glorious presence without fault and with great joy, to the only God our Savior be glory, majesty, power and authority, through Jesus Christ our Lord, before all ages, now and forevermore ! Amen

If You would like to contact Jerry Moses or support his ministry in anyway, you may reach him at this email address:

Divineinterventionjm3722@yahoo.com

If You have never personally invited Jesus Christ (The SON of GOD) into your heart, to take over your life, turning the wrong into right, and making a way where there seems to be no way, then NOW is a good time to start.

Jesus Christ, an innocent man, was tortured and died for OUR sins, so we could repent and choose to not repeat purposeful sin. HE paid a high price so YOU can spend eternity with HIM in heaven.

JUST BELIEVE!!! Get a Bible, and start reading it each day, pray to God in Jesus name and ask the powerful Holy Spirit to guide you to live right according to Heaven's rules! Its that easy!

Prayer this prayer and KNOW GOD will immediately write your name in the Lamb's Book of Life, and begin working on your loved ones as well.

PRAY....

Lord Jesus, forgive me of my sins, I believe you died for me and rose the third day, I repent of all my sins and choose to live to please You LORD.

Holy Spirit remove from my life what should not be there and add what should. Heal me inside and out, deliver me from all evil, and help save my loved ones too. In Jesus name I pray, AMEN.

Revelation 20:15

And who's ever name is not found written in the Lamb's Book of Life will be thrown into the Lake of Fire.

Revelation 3:5 They that overcome (purposeful sin), the same will be clothed in white raiment; and I the LORD, will NOT blot out their name from the Lamb's Book of Life, but I will confess their name before my Father, and before his angels.

www.ingramcontent.com/pod-product-compliance
Lightning Source LLC
Chambersburg PA
CBHW021110130626

46554CB00002B/616